AI
Self-Driving Cars
Vicissitude

Practical Advances in
Artificial Intelligence and Machine Learning

Dr. Lance B. Eliot, MBA, PhD

DEDICATION

To my incredible daughter, Lauren, and my incredible son, Michael.

Forest fortuna adiuvat (from the Latin; good fortune favors the brave).

DEDICATION

To my incredible daughter, Lauren, and my incredible son, Michael.
Forest fortuna adiuvat (from the Latin; good fortune favors the brave).

CONTENTS

ACKNOWLEDGMENTS

I have been the beneficiary of advice and counsel by many friends, colleagues, family, investors, and many others. I want to thank everyone that has aided me throughout my career. I write from the heart and the head, having experienced first-hand what it means to have others around you that support you during the good times and the tough times.

To Warren Bennis, one of my doctoral advisors and ultimately a colleague, I offer my deepest thanks and appreciation, especially for his calm and insightful wisdom and support.

To Mark Stevens and his generous efforts toward funding and supporting the USC Stevens Center for Innovation.

To Lloyd Greif and the USC Lloyd Greif Center for Entrepreneurial Studies for their ongoing encouragement of founders and entrepreneurs.

To Peter Drucker, William Wang, Aaron Levie, Peter Kim, Jon Kraft, Cindy Crawford, Jenny Ming, Steve Milligan, Chis Underwood, Frank Gehry, Buzz Aldrin, Steve Forbes, Bill Thompson, Dave Dillon, Alan Fuerstman, Larry Ellison, Jim Sinegal, John Sperling, Mark Stevenson, Anand Nallathambi, Thomas Barrack, Jr., and many other innovators and leaders that I have met and gained mightily from doing so.

Thanks to Ed Trainor, Kevin Anderson, James Hickey, Wendell Jones, Ken Harris, DuWayne Peterson, Mike Brown, Jim Thornton, Abhi Beniwal, Al Biland, John Nomura, Eliot Weinman, John Desmond, and many others for their unwavering support during my career.

And most of all thanks as always to Lauren and Michael, for their ongoing support and for having seen me writing and heard much of this material during the many months involved in writing it. To their patience and willingness to listen.

INTRODUCTION

This is a book that provides the newest innovations and the latest Artificial Intelligence (AI) advances about the emerging nature of AI-based autonomous self-driving driverless cars. Via recent advances in Artificial Intelligence (AI) and Machine Learning (ML), we are nearing the day when vehicles can control themselves and will not require and nor rely upon human intervention to perform their driving tasks (or, that <u>allow</u> for human intervention, but only *require* human intervention in very limited ways).

Similar to my other related books, which I describe in a moment and list the chapters in the Appendix A of this book, I am particularly focused on those advances that pertain to self-driving cars. The phrase "autonomous vehicles" is often used to refer to any kind of vehicle, whether it is ground-based or in the air or sea, and whether it is a cargo hauling trailer truck or a conventional passenger car. Though the aspects described in this book are certainly applicable to all kinds of autonomous vehicles, I am focused more so here on cars.

Indeed, I am especially known for my role in aiding the advancement of self-driving cars, serving currently as the Executive Director of the Cybernetic AI Self-Driving Cars Institute. In addition to writing software, designing and developing systems and software for self-driving cars, I also speak and write quite a bit about the topic. This book is a collection of some of my more advanced essays. For those of you that might have seen my essays posted elsewhere, I have updated them and integrated them into this book as one handy cohesive package.

You might be interested in companion books that I have written that provide additional key innovations and fundamentals about self-driving cars. Those books are entitled **"Introduction to Driverless Self-Driving Cars," "Advances in AI and Autonomous Vehicles: Cybernetic Self-Driving Cars," "Self-Driving Cars: "The Mother of All AI Projects," "Innovation and Thought Leadership on Self-Driving Driverless Cars," "New Advances in AI Autonomous Driverless Self-Driving Cars," "Autonomous Vehicle Driverless Self-Driving Cars and Artificial Intelligence," "Transformative Artificial Intelligence**

Driverless Self-Driving Cars," "Disruptive Artificial Intelligence and Driverless Self-Driving Cars, and "State-of-the-Art AI Driverless Self-Driving Cars," and "Top Trends in AI Self-Driving Cars," and "AI Innovations and Self-Driving Cars," "Crucial Advances for AI Driverless Cars," "Sociotechnical Insights and AI Driverless Cars," "Pioneering Advances for AI Driverless Cars" and "Leading Edge Trends for AI Driverless Cars," "The Cutting Edge of AI Autonomous Cars" and "The Next Wave of AI Self-Driving Cars" and "Revolutionary Innovations of AI Self-Driving Cars," and "AI Self-Driving Cars Breakthroughs," "Trailblazing Trends for AI Self-Driving Cars," "Ingenious Strides for AI Driverless Cars," "AI Self-Driving Cars Inventiveness," "Visionary Secrets of AI Driverless Cars," "Spearheading AI Self-Driving Cars," "Spurring AI Self-Driving Cars," "Avant-Garde AI Driverless Cars," "AI Self-Driving Cars Evolvement," "AI Driverless Cars Chrysalis," "Boosting AI Autonomous Cars," "AI Self-Driving Cars Trendsetting," "AI Autonomous Cars Forefront, "AI Autonomous Cars Emergence," "AI Autonomous Cars Progress," "AI Self-Driving Cars Prognosis," "AI Self-Driving Cars Momentum," "AI Self-Driving Cars Headway," "AI Self-Driving Cars Vicissitude" (they are available on Amazon).

For this book, I am going to borrow my introduction from those companion books, since it does a good job of laying out the landscape of self-driving cars and my overall viewpoints on the topic. The remainder of this book is material that does not appear in the companion books.

INTRODUCTION TO SELF-DRIVING CARS

This is a book about self-driving cars. Someday in the future, we'll all have self-driving cars and this book will perhaps seem antiquated, but right now, we are at the forefront of the self-driving car wave. Daily news bombards us with flashes of new announcements by one car maker or another and leaves the impression that within the next few weeks or maybe months that the self-driving car will be here. A casual non-technical reader would assume from these news flashes that in fact we must be on the cusp of a true self-driving car. Here's a real news flash: We are still quite a distance from having a true self-driving car. It is years to go before we get there.

A true self-driving car is akin to a moonshot. In the same manner that getting us to the moon was an incredible feat, likewise, is achieving a true self-driving car. Anybody that suggests or even brashly states that the true self-driving car is nearly here should be viewed with great skepticism. Indeed, you'll see that I often tend to use the word "hogwash" or "crock" when I assess much of the decidedly *fake news* about self-driving cars.

Indeed, I've been writing a popular blog post about self-driving cars and hitting hard on those that try to wave their hands and pretend that we are on the imminent verge of true self-driving cars. For many years, I've been known as the AI Insider. Besides writing about AI, I also develop AI software. I do what I describe. It also gives me insights into what others that are doing AI are really doing versus what it is said they are doing.

Many faithful readers had asked me to pull together my insightful short essays and put them into another book, which you are now holding.

For those of you that have been reading my essays over the years, this collection not only puts them together into one handy package, I also updated the essays and added new material. For those of you that are new to the topic of self-driving cars and AI, I hope you find these essays approachable and informative. I also tend to have a writing style with a bit of a voice, and so you'll see that I am times have a wry sense of humor and poke at conformity.

As a former professor and founder of an AI research lab, I for many years wrote in the formal language of academic writing. I published in referred journals and served as an editor for several AI journals. This writing here is not of the nature, and I have adopted a different and more informal style for these essays. That being said, I also do mention from time-to-time more rigorous material on AI and encourage you all to dig into those deeper and more formal materials if so interested.

I am also an AI practitioner. This means that I write AI software for a living. Currently, I head-up the Cybernetics Self-Driving Car Institute, where we are developing AI software for self-driving cars. I am excited to also report that my son, also a software engineer, heads-up our Cybernetics Self-Driving Car Lab. What I have helped to start, and for which he is an integral part, ultimately he will carry long into the future after I have retired. My daughter, a marketing whiz, also is integral to our efforts as head of our Marketing group. She too will carry forward the legacy now being formulated.

For those of you that are reading this book and have a penchant for writing code, you might consider taking a look at the open source code available for self-driving cars. This is a handy place to start learning how to develop AI for self-driving cars. There are also many new educational courses spring forth. There is a growing body of those wanting to learn about and develop self-driving cars, and a growing body of colleges, labs, and other avenues by which you can learn about self-driving cars.

This book will provide a foundation of aspects that I think will get you ready for those kinds of more advanced training opportunities. If you've already taken those classes, you'll likely find these essays especially interesting as they offer a perspective that I am betting few other instructors or faculty offered to you. These are challenging essays that ask you to think beyond the conventional about self-driving cars.

3

THE MOTHER OF ALL AI PROJECTS

In June 2017, Apple CEO Tim Cook came out and finally admitted that Apple has been working on a self-driving car. As you'll see in my essays, Apple was enmeshed in secrecy about their self-driving car efforts. We have only been able to read the tea leaves and guess at what Apple has been up to. The notion of an iCar has been floating for quite a while, and self-driving engineers and researchers have been signing tight-lipped Non-Disclosure Agreements (NDA's) to work on projects at Apple that were as shrouded in mystery as any military invasion plans might be.

Tim Cook said something that many others in the Artificial Intelligence (AI) field have been saying, namely, the creation of a self-driving car has got to be the mother of all AI projects. In other words, it is in fact a tremendous moonshot for AI. If a self-driving car can be crafted and the AI works as we hope, it means that we have made incredible strides with AI and that therefore it opens many other worlds of potential breakthrough accomplishments that AI can solve.

Is this hyperbole? Am I just trying to make AI seem like a miracle worker and so provide self-aggrandizing statements for those of us writing the AI software for self-driving cars? No, it is not hyperbole. Developing a true self-driving car is really, really, really hard to do. Let me take a moment to explain why. As a side note, I realize that the Apple CEO is known for at times uttering hyperbole, and he had previously said for example that the year 2012 was "the mother of all years," and he had said that the release of iOS 10 was "the mother of all releases" – all of which does suggest he likes to use the handy "mother of" expression. But, I assure you, in terms of true self-driving cars, he has hit the nail on the head. For sure.

When you think about a moonshot and how we got to the moon, there are some identifiable characteristics and those same aspects can be applied to creating a true self-driving car. You'll notice that I keep putting the word "true" in front of the self-driving car expression. I do so because as per my essay about the various levels of self-driving cars, there are some self-driving cars that are only somewhat of a self-driving car. The somewhat versions are ones that require a human driver to be ready to intervene. In my view, that's not a true self-driving car. A true self-driving car is one that requires no human driver intervention at all. It is a car that can entirely undertake via automation the driving task without any human driver needed. This is the essence of what is known as a Level 5 self-driving car. We are currently at the Level 2 and Level 3 mark, and not yet at Level 5.

Getting to the moon involved aspects such as having big stretch goals, incremental progress, experimentation, innovation, and so on. Let's review how this applied to the moonshot of the bygone era, and how it applies to the self-driving car moonshot of today.

Big Stretch Goal

Trying to take a human and deliver the human to the moon, and bring them back, safely, was an extremely large stretch goal at the time. No one knew whether it could be done. The technology wasn't available yet. The cost was huge. The determination would need to be fierce. Etc. To reach a Level 5 self-driving car is going to be the same. It is a big stretch goal. We can readily get to the Level 3, and we are able to see the Level 4 just up ahead, but a Level 5 is still an unknown as to if it is doable. It should eventually be doable and in the same way that we thought we'd eventually get to the moon, but when it will occur is a different story.

Incremental Progress

Getting to the moon did not happen overnight in one fell swoop. It took years and years of incremental progress to get there. Likewise for self-driving cars. Google has famously been striving to get to the Level 5, and pretty much been willing to forgo dealing with the intervening levels, but most of the other self-driving car makers are doing the incremental route. Let's get a good Level 2 and a somewhat Level 3 going. Then, let's improve the Level 3 and get a somewhat Level 4 going. Then, let's improve the Level 4 and finally arrive at a Level 5. This seems to be the prevalent way that we are going to achieve the true self-driving car.

Experimentation

You likely know that there were various experiments involved in perfecting the approach and technology to get to the moon. As per making incremental progress, we first tried to see if we could get a rocket to go into space and safety return, then put a monkey in there, then with a human, then we went all the way to the moon but didn't land, and finally we arrived at the mission that actually landed on the moon. Self-driving cars are the same way. We are doing simulations of self-driving cars. We do testing of self-driving cars on private land under controlled situations. We do testing of self-driving cars on public roadways, often having to meet regulatory requirements including for example having an engineer or equivalent in the car to take over the controls if needed. And so on. Experiments big and small are needed to figure out what works and what doesn't.

Innovation

There are already some advances in AI that are allowing us to progress toward self-driving cars. We are going to need even more advances. Innovation in all aspects of technology are going to be required to achieve a true self-driving car. By no means do we already have everything in-hand that we need to get there. Expect new inventions and new approaches, new algorithms, etc.

Setbacks

Most of the pundits are avoiding talking about potential setbacks in the progress toward self-driving cars. Getting to the moon involved many setbacks, some of which you never have heard of and were buried at the time so as to not dampen enthusiasm and funding for getting to the moon. A recurring theme in many of my included essays is that there are going to be setbacks as we try to arrive at a true self-driving car. Take a deep breath and be ready. I just hope the setbacks don't completely stop progress. I am sure that it will cause progress to alter in a manner that we've not yet seen in the self-driving car field. I liken the self-driving car of today to the excitement everyone had for Uber when it first got going. Today, we have a different view of Uber and with each passing day there are more regulations to the ride sharing business and more concerns raised. The darling child only stays a darling until finally that child acts up. It will happen the same with self-driving cars.

SELF-DRIVING CARS CHALLENGES

But what exactly makes things so hard to have a true self-driving car, you might be asking. You have seen cruise control for years and years. You've lately seen cars that can do parallel parking. You've seen YouTube videos of Tesla drivers that put their hands out the window as their car zooms along the highway, and seen to therefore be in a self-driving car. Aren't we just needing to put a few more sensors onto a car and then we'll have in-hand a true self-driving car? Nope.

Consider for a moment the nature of the driving task. We don't just let anyone at any age drive a car. Worldwide, most countries won't license a driver until the age of 18, though many do allow a learner's permit at the age of 15 or 16. Some suggest that a younger age would be physically too small to reach the controls of the car. Though this might be the case, we could easily adjust the controls to allow for younger aged and thus smaller stature. It's not their physical size that matters. It's their cognitive development that matters.

To drive a car, you need to be able to reason about the car, what the car can and cannot do. You need to know how to operate the car. You need to know about how other cars on the road drive. You need to know what is allowed in driving such as speed limits and driving within marked lanes. You need to be able to react to situations and be able to avoid getting into accidents. You need to ascertain when to hit your brakes, when to steer clear of a pedestrian, and how to keep from ramming that motorcyclist that just cut you off.

Many of us had taken courses on driving. We studied about driving and took driver training. We had to take a test and pass it to be able to drive. The point being that though most adults take the driving task for granted, and we often "mindlessly" drive our cars, there is a significant amount of cognitive effort that goes into driving a car. After a while, it becomes second nature. You don't especially think about how you drive, you just do it. But, if you watch a novice driver, say a teenager learning to drive, you suddenly realize that there is a lot more complexity to it than we seem to realize.

Furthermore, driving is a very serious task. I recall when my daughter and son first learned to drive. They are both very conscientious people. They wanted to make sure that whatever they did, they did well, and that they did not harm anyone. Every day, when you get into a car, it is probably around 4,000 pounds of hefty metal and plastics (about two tons), and it is a lethal weapon. Think about it. You drive down the street in an object that weighs two tons and with the engine it can accelerate and ram into anything you want to hit. The damage a car can inflict is very scary. Both my children were surprised that they were being given the right to maneuver this monster of a beast that could cause tremendous harm entirely by merely letting go of the steering wheel for a moment or taking your eyes off the road.

In fact, in the United States alone there are about 30,000 deaths per year by auto accidents, which is around 100 per day. Given that there are about 263 million cars in the United States, I am actually more amazed that the number of fatalities is not a lot higher. During my morning commute, I look at all the thousands of cars on the freeway around me, and I think that if all of them decided to go zombie and drive in a crazy maniac way, there would be many people dead. Somehow, incredibly, each day, most people drive relatively safely. To me, that's a miracle right there. Getting millions and millions of people to be safe and sane when behind the wheel of a two ton mobile object, it's a feat that we as a society should admire with pride.

So, hopefully you are in agreement that the driving task requires a great deal of cognition. You don't' need to be especially smart to drive a car, and we've done quite a bit to make car driving viable for even the average dolt. There isn't an IQ test that you need to take to drive a car. If you can read and write, and pass a test, you pretty much can legally drive a car. There are of course some that drive a car and are not legally permitted to do so, plus there are private areas such as farms where drivers are young, but for public roadways in the United States, you can be generally of average intelligence (or less) and be able to legally drive.

This though makes it seem like the cognitive effort must not be much. If the cognitive effort was truly hard, wouldn't we only have Einstein's that could drive a car? We have made sure to keep the driving task as simple as we can, by making the controls easy and relatively standardized, and by having roads that are relatively standardized, and so on. It is as though Disneyland has put their Autopia into the real-world, by us all as a society agreeing that roads will be a certain way, and we'll all abide by the various rules of driving.

A modest cognitive task by a human is still something that stymies AI. You certainly know that AI has been able to beat chess players and be good at other kinds of games. This type of narrow cognition is not what car driving is about. Car driving is much wider. It requires knowledge about the world, which a chess playing AI system does not need to know. The cognitive aspects of driving are on the one hand seemingly simple, but at the same time require layer upon layer of knowledge about cars, people, roads, rules, and a myriad of other "common sense" aspects. We don't have any AI systems today that have that same kind of breadth and depth of awareness and knowledge.

As revealed in my essays, the self-driving car of today is using trickery to do particular tasks. It is all very narrow in operation. Plus, it currently assumes that a human driver is ready to intervene. It is like a child that we have taught to stack blocks, but we are needed to be right there in case the child stacks them too high and they begin to fall over. AI of today is brittle, it is narrow, and it does not approach the cognitive abilities of humans. This is why the true self-driving car is somewhere out in the future.

Another aspect to the driving task is that it is not solely a mind exercise. You do need to use your senses to drive. You use your eyes a vision sensors to see the road ahead. You vision capability is like a streaming video, which your brain needs to continually analyze as you drive. Where is the road? Is there a pedestrian in the way? Is there another car ahead of you? Your senses are relying a flood of info to your brain. Self-driving cars are trying to do the same, by using cameras, radar, ultrasound, and lasers. This is an attempt at mimicking how humans have senses and sensory apparatus.

Thus, the driving task is mental and physical. You use your senses, you use your arms and legs to manipulate the controls of the car, and you use your brain to assess the sensory info and direct your limbs to act upon the controls of the car. This all happens instantly. If you've ever perhaps gotten something in your eye and only had one eye available to drive with, you suddenly realize how dependent upon vision you are. If you have a broken foot with a cast, you suddenly realize how hard it is to control the brake pedal and the accelerator. If you've taken medication and your brain is maybe sluggish, you suddenly realize how much mental strain is required to drive a car.

An AI system that plays chess only needs to be focused on playing chess. The physical aspects aren't important because usually a human moves the chess pieces or the chessboard is shown on an electronic display. Using AI for a more life-and-death task such as analyzing MRI images of patients, this again does not require physical capabilities and instead is done by examining images of bits.

Driving a car is a true life-and-death task. It is a use of AI that can easily and at any moment produce death. For those colleagues of mine that are developing this AI, as am I, we need to keep in mind the somber aspects of this. We are producing software that will have in its virtual hands the lives of the occupants of the car, and the lives of those in other nearby cars, and the lives of nearby pedestrians, etc. Chess is not usually a life-or-death matter.

Driving is all around us. Cars are everywhere. Most of today's AI applications involve only a small number of people. Or, they are behind the scenes and we as humans have other recourse if the AI messes up. AI that is driving a car at 80 miles per hour on a highway had better not mess up. The consequences are grave. Multiply this by the number of cars, if we could put magically self-driving into every car in the USA, we'd have AI running in the 263 million cars. That's a lot of AI spread around. This is AI on a massive scale that we are not doing today and that offers both promise and potential peril.

There are some that want AI for self-driving cars because they envision a world without any car accidents. They envision a world in which there is no car congestion and all cars cooperate with each other. These are wonderful utopian visions.

They are also very misleading. The adoption of self-driving cars is going to be incremental and not overnight. We cannot economically just junk all existing cars. Nor are we going to be able to affordably retrofit existing cars. It is more likely that self-driving cars will be built into new cars and that over many years of gradual replacement of existing cars that we'll see the mix of self-driving cars become substantial in the real-world.

In these essays, I have tried to offer technological insights without being overly technical in my description, and also blended the business, societal, and economic aspects too. Technologists need to consider the non-technological impacts of what they do. Non-technologists should be aware of what is being developed.

We all need to work together to collectively be prepared for the enormous disruption and transformative aspects of true self-driving cars. We all need to be involved in this mother of all AI projects.

WHAT THIS BOOK PROVIDES

What does this book provide to you? It introduces many of the key elements about self-driving cars and does so with an AI based perspective. I weave together technical and non-technical aspects, readily going from being concerned about the cognitive capabilities of the driving task and how the technology is embodying this into self-driving cars, and in the next breath I discuss the societal and economic aspects.

They are all intertwined because that's the way reality is. You cannot separate out the technology per se, and instead must consider it within the milieu of what is being invented and innovated, and do so with a mindset towards the contemporary mores and culture that shape what we are doing and what we hope to do.

WHY THIS BOOK

I wrote this book to try and bring to the public view many aspects about self-driving cars that nobody seems to be discussing.

For business leaders that are either involved in making self-driving cars or that are going to leverage self-driving cars, I hope that this book will enlighten you as to the risks involved and ways in which you should be strategizing about how to deal with those risks.

For entrepreneurs, startups and other businesses that want to enter into the self-driving car market that is emerging, I hope this book sparks your interest in doing so, and provides some sense of what might be prudent to pursue.

For researchers that study self-driving cars, I hope this book spurs your interest in the risks and safety issues of self-driving cars, and also nudges you toward conducting research on those aspects.

For students in computer science or related disciplines, I hope this book will provide you with interesting and new ideas and material, for which you might conduct research or provide some career direction insights for you.

For AI companies and high-tech companies pursuing self-driving cars, this book will hopefully broaden your view beyond just the mere coding and development needed to make self-driving cars.

For all readers, I hope that you will find the material in this book to be stimulating. Some of it will be repetitive of things you already know. But I am pretty sure that you'll also find various eureka moments whereby you'll discover a new technique or approach that you had not earlier thought of. I am also betting that there will be material that forces you to rethink some of your current practices.

I am not saying you will suddenly have an epiphany and change what you are doing. I do think though that you will reconsider or perhaps revisit what you are doing.

For anyone choosing to use this book for teaching purposes, please take a look at my suggestions for doing so, as described in the Appendix. I have found the material handy in courses that I have taught, and likewise other faculty have told me that they have found the material handy, in some cases as extended readings and in other instances as a core part of their course (depending on the nature of the class).

In my writing for this book, I have tried carefully to blend both the practitioner and the academic styles of writing. It is not as dense as is typical academic journal writing, but at the same time offers depth by going into the nuances and trade-offs of various practices.

The word "deep" is in vogue today, meaning getting deeply into a subject or topic, and so is the word "unpack" which means to tease out the underlying aspects of a subject or topic. I have sought to offer material that addresses an issue or topic by going relatively deeply into it and make sure that it is well unpacked.

In any book about AI, it is difficult to use our everyday words without having some of them be misinterpreted. Specifically, it is easy to anthropomorphize AI. When I say that an AI system "knows" something, I do not want you to construe that the AI system has sentience and "knows" in the same way that humans do. They aren't that way, as yet. I have tried to use quotes around such words from time-to-time to emphasize that the words I am using should not be misinterpreted to ascribe true human intelligence to the AI systems that we know of today. If I used quotes around all such words, the book would be very difficult to read, and so I am doing so judiciously. Please keep that in mind as you read the material, thanks.

Some of the material is time-based in terms of covering underway activities, and though some of it might decay, nonetheless I believe you'll find the material useful and informative.

COMPANION BOOKS

1. **"Introduction to Driverless Self-Driving Cars"** by Dr. Lance Eliot
2. **"Innovation and Thought Leadership on Self-Driving Driverless Cars"** by Dr. Lance Eliot
3. **"Advances in AI and Autonomous Vehicles: Cybernetic Self-Driving Cars"** by Dr. Lance Eliot
4. **"Self-Driving Cars: The Mother of All AI Projects"** by Dr. Lance Eliot
5. **"New Advances in AI Autonomous Driverless Self-Driving Cars"** by Dr. Lance Eliot
6. **"Autonomous Vehicle Driverless Self-Driving Cars and Artificial Intelligence"** by Dr. Lance Eliot and Michael B. Eliot
7. **"Transformative Artificial Intelligence Driverless Self-Driving Cars"** by Dr. Lance Eliot
8. **"Disruptive Artificial Intelligence and Driverless Self-Driving Cars"** by Dr. Lance Eliot
9. "State-of-the-Art AI Driverless Self-Driving Cars" by Dr. Lance Eliot
10. **"Top Trends in AI Self-Driving Cars"** by Dr. Lance Eliot
11. **"AI Innovations and Self-Driving Cars"** by Dr. Lance Eliot
12. **"Crucial Advances for AI Driverless Cars"** by Dr. Lance Eliot
13. **"Sociotechnical Insights and AI Driverless Cars"** by Dr. Lance Eliot.
14. **"Pioneering Advances for AI Driverless Cars"** by Dr. Lance Eliot
15. **"Leading Edge Trends for AI Driverless Cars"** by Dr. Lance Eliot
16. **"The Cutting Edge of AI Autonomous Cars"** by Dr. Lance Eliot
17. **"The Next Wave of AI Self-Driving Cars"** by Dr. Lance Eliot
18. **"Revolutionary Innovations of AI Driverless Cars"** by Dr. Lance Eliot
19. **"AI Self-Driving Cars Breakthroughs"** by Dr. Lance Eliot
20. **"Trailblazing Trends for AI Self-Driving Cars"** by Dr. Lance Eliot
21. **"Ingenious Strides for AI Driverless Cars"** by Dr. Lance Eliot
22. **"AI Self-Driving Cars Inventiveness"** by Dr. Lance Eliot
23. **"Visionary Secrets of AI Driverless Cars"** by Dr. Lance Eliot
24. **"Spearheading AI Self-Driving Cars"** by Dr. Lance Eliot
25. **"Spurring AI Self-Driving Cars"** by Dr. Lance Eliot
26. **"Avant-Garde AI Driverless Cars"** by Dr. Lance Eliot
27. **"AI Self-Driving Cars Evolvement"** by Dr. Lance Eliot
28. **"AI Driverless Cars Chrysalis"** by Dr. Lance Eliot
29. **"Boosting AI Autonomous Cars"** by Dr. Lance Eliot
30. **"AI Self-Driving Cars Trendsetting"** by Dr. Lance Eliot
31. **"AI Autonomous Cars Forefront"** by Dr. Lance Eliot
32. **"AI Autonomous Cars Emergence"** by Dr. Lance Eliot
33. **"AI Autonomous Cars Progress"** by Dr. Lance Eliot
34. **"AI Self-Driving Cars Prognosis"** by Dr. Lance Eliot
35. **"AI Self-Driving Cars Momentum"** by Dr. Lance Eliot
36. **"AI Self-Driving Cars Headway"** by Dr. Lance Eliot
37. **"AI Self-Driving Cars Vicissitude"** by Dr. Lance Eliot

These books are available on Amazon and at other major global booksellers.

CHAPTER 1

ELIOT FRAMEWORK FOR AI SELF-DRIVING CARS

CHAPTER 1

ELIOT FRAMEWORK FOR AI SELF-DRIVING CARS

This chapter is a core foundational aspect for understanding AI self-driving cars and I have used this same chapter in several of my other books to introduce the reader to essential elements of this field. Once you've read this chapter, you'll be prepared to read the rest of the material since the foundational essence of the components of autonomous AI driverless self-driving cars will have been established for you.

———————

When I give presentations about self-driving cars and teach classes on the topic, I have found it helpful to provide a framework around which the various key elements of self-driving cars can be understood and organized (see diagram at the end of this chapter). The framework needs to be simple enough to convey the overarching elements, but at the same time not so simple that it belies the true complexity of self-driving cars. As such, I am going to describe the framework here and try to offer in a thousand words (or more!) what the framework diagram itself intends to portray.

The core elements on the diagram are numbered for ease of reference. The numbering does not suggest any kind of prioritization of the elements. Each element is crucial. Each element has a purpose, and otherwise would not be included in the framework. For some self-driving cars, a particular element might be more important or somehow distinguished in comparison to other self-driving cars.

You could even use the framework to rate a particular self-driving car, doing so by gauging how well it performs in each of the elements of the framework. I will describe each of the elements, one at a time. After doing so, I'll discuss aspects that illustrate how the elements interact and perform during the overall effort of a self-driving car.

At the Cybernetic Self-Driving Car Institute, we use the framework to keep track of what we are working on, and how we are developing software that fills in what is needed to achieve Level 5 self-driving cars.

D-01: Sensor Capture

Let's start with the one element that often gets the most attention in the press about self-driving cars, namely, the sensory devices for a self-driving car.

On the framework, the box labeled as D-01 indicates "Sensor Capture" and refers to the processes of the self-driving car that involve collecting data from the myriad of sensors that are used for a self-driving car. The types of devices typically involved are listed, such as the use of mono cameras, stereo cameras, LIDAR devices, radar systems, ultrasonic devices, GPS, IMU, and so on.

These devices are tasked with obtaining data about the status of the self-driving car and the world around it. Some of the devices are continually providing updates, while others of the devices await an indication by the self-driving car that the device is supposed to collect data. The data might be first transformed in some fashion by the device itself, or it might instead be fed directly into the sensor capture as raw data. At that point, it might be up to the sensor capture processes to do transformations on the data. This all varies depending upon the nature of the devices being used and how the devices were designed and developed.

D-02: Sensor Fusion

Imagine that your eyeballs receive visual images, your nose receives odors, your ears receive sounds, and in essence each of your distinct sensory devices is getting some form of input. The input befits the nature of the device. Likewise, for a self-driving car, the cameras provide visual images, the radar returns radar reflections, and so on.

Each device provides the data as befits what the device does.

At some point, using the analogy to humans, you need to merge together what your eyes see, what your nose smells, what your ears hear, and piece it all together into a larger sense of what the world is all about and what is happening around you. Sensor fusion is the action of taking the singular aspects from each of the devices and putting them together into a larger puzzle.

Sensor fusion is a tough task. There are some devices that might not be working at the time of the sensor capture. Or, there might some devices that are unable to report well what they have detected. Again, using a human analogy, suppose you are in a dark room and so your eyes cannot see much. At that point, you might need to rely more so on your ears and what you hear. The same is true for a self-driving car. If the cameras are obscured due to snow and sleet, it might be that the radar can provide a greater indication of what the external conditions consist of.

In the case of a self-driving car, there can be a plethora of such sensory devices. Each is reporting what it can. Each might have its difficulties. Each might have its limitations, such as how far ahead it can detect an object. All of these limitations need to be considered during the sensor fusion task.

D-03: Virtual World Model

For humans, we presumably keep in our minds a model of the world around us when we are driving a car. In your mind, you know that the car is going at say 60 miles per hour and that you are on a freeway. You have a model in your mind that your car is surrounded by other cars, and that there are lanes to the freeway. Your model is not only based on what you can see, hear, etc., but also what you know about the nature of the world. You know that at any moment that car ahead of you can smash on its brakes, or the car behind you can ram into your car, or that the truck in the next lane might swerve into your lane.

The AI of the self-driving car needs to have a virtual world model, which it then keeps updated with whatever it is receiving from the sensor fusion, which received its input from the sensor capture and the sensory devices.

D-04: System Action Plan

By having a virtual world model, the AI of the self-driving car is able to keep track of where the car is and what is happening around the car. In addition, the AI needs to determine what to do next. Should the self-driving car hit its brakes? Should the self-driving car stay in its lane or swerve into the lane to the left? Should the self-driving car accelerate or slow down?

A system action plan needs to be prepared by the AI of the self-driving car. The action plan specifies what actions should be taken. The actions need to pertain to the status of the virtual world model. Plus, the actions need to be realizable.

This realizability means that the AI cannot just assert that the self-driving car should suddenly sprout wings and fly. Instead, the AI must be bound by whatever the self-driving car can actually do, such as coming to a halt in a distance of X feet at a speed of Y miles per hour, rather than perhaps asserting that the self-driving car come to a halt in 0 feet as though it could instantaneously come to a stop while it is in motion.

D-05: Controls Activation

The system action plan is implemented by activating the controls of the car to act according to what the plan stipulates. This might mean that the accelerator control is commanded to increase the speed of the car. Or, the steering control is commanded to turn the steering wheel 30 degrees to the left or right.

One question arises as to whether or not the controls respond as they are commanded to do. In other words, suppose the AI has commanded the accelerator to increase, but for some reason it does not do so. Or, maybe it tries to do so, but the speed of the car does not increase. The controls activation feeds back into the virtual world model, and simultaneously the virtual world model is getting updated from the sensors, the sensor capture, and the sensor fusion. This allows the AI to ascertain what has taken place as a result of the controls being commanded to take some kind of action.

By the way, please keep in mind that though the diagram seems to have a linear progression to it, the reality is that these are all aspects of the self-driving car that are happening in parallel and simultaneously. The sensors are capturing data, meanwhile the sensor fusion is taking place, meanwhile the virtual model is being updated, meanwhile the system action plan is being formulated and reformulated, meanwhile the controls are being activated.

This is the same as a human being that is driving a car. They are eyeballing the road, meanwhile they are fusing in their mind the sights, sounds, etc., meanwhile their mind is updating their model of the world around them, meanwhile they are formulating an action plan of what to do, and meanwhile they are pushing their foot onto the pedals and steering the car. In the normal course of driving a car, you are doing all of these at once. I mention this so that when you look at the diagram, you will think of the boxes as processes that are all happening at the same time, and not as though only one happens and then the next.

They are shown diagrammatically in a simplistic manner to help comprehend what is taking place. You though should also realize that they are working in parallel and simultaneous with each other. This is a tough aspect in that the inter-element communications involve latency and other aspects that must be taken into account. There can be delays in one element updating and then sharing its latest status with other elements.

D-06: Automobile & CAN

Contemporary cars use various automotive electronics and a Controller Area Network (CAN) to serve as the components that underlie the driving aspects of a car. There are Electronic Control Units (ECU's) which control subsystems of the car, such as the engine, the brakes, the doors, the windows, and so on.

The elements D-01, D-02, D-03, D-04, D-05 are layered on top of the D-06, and must be aware of the nature of what the D-06 is able to do and not do.

D-07: In-Car Commands

Humans are going to be occupants in self-driving cars. In a Level 5 self-driving car, there must be some form of communication that takes place between the humans and the self-driving car. For example, I go into a self-driving car and tell it that I want to be driven over to Disneyland, and along the way I want to stop at In-and-Out Burger. The self-driving car now parses what I've said and tries to then establish a means to carry out my wishes.

In-car commands can happen at any time during a driving journey. Though my example was about an in-car command when I first got into my self-driving car, it could be that while the self-driving car is carrying out the journey that I change my mind. Perhaps after getting stuck in traffic, I tell the self-driving car to forget about getting the burgers and just head straight over to the theme park. The self-driving car needs to be alert to in-car commands throughout the journey.

D-08: V2X Communications

We will ultimately have self-driving cars communicating with each other, doing so via V2V (Vehicle-to-Vehicle) communications. We will also have self-driving cars that communicate with the roadways and other aspects of the transportation infrastructure, doing so via V2I (Vehicle-to-Infrastructure).

The variety of ways in which a self-driving car will be communicating with other cars and infrastructure is being called V2X, whereby the letter X means whatever else we identify as something that a car should or would want to communicate with. The V2X communications will be taking place simultaneous with everything else on the diagram, and those other elements will need to incorporate whatever it gleans from those V2X communications.

D-09: Deep Learning

The use of Deep Learning permeates all other aspects of the self-driving car. The AI of the self-driving car will be using deep learning to do a better job at the systems action plan, and at the controls activation, and at the sensor fusion, and so on.

Currently, the use of artificial neural networks is the most prevalent form of deep learning. Based on large swaths of data, the neural networks attempt to "learn" from the data and therefore direct the efforts of the self-driving car accordingly.

D-10: Tactical AI

Tactical AI is the element of dealing with the moment-to-moment driving of the self-driving car. Is the self-driving car staying in its lane of the freeway? Is the car responding appropriately to the controls commands? Are the sensory devices working?

For human drivers, the tactical equivalent can be seen when you watch a novice driver such as a teenager that is first driving. They are focused on the mechanics of the driving task, keeping their eye on the road while also trying to properly control the car.

D-11: Strategic AI

The Strategic AI aspects of a self-driving car are dealing with the larger picture of what the self-driving car is trying to do. If I had asked that the self-driving car take me to Disneyland, there is an overall journey map that needs to be kept and maintained.

There is an interaction between the Strategic AI and the Tactical AI. The Strategic AI is wanting to keep on the mission of the driving, while the Tactical AI is focused on the particulars underway in the driving effort. If the Tactical AI seems to wander away from the overarching mission, the Strategic AI wants to see why and get things back on track. If the Tactical AI realizes that there is something amiss on the self-driving car, it needs to alert the Strategic AI accordingly and have an adjustment to the overarching mission that is underway.

D-12: Self-Aware AI

Very few of the self-driving cars being developed are including a Self-Aware AI element, which we at the Cybernetic Self-Driving Car Institute believe is crucial to Level 5 self-driving cars.

The Self-Aware AI element is intended to watch over itself, in the sense that the AI is making sure that the AI is working as intended. Suppose you had a human driving a car, and they were starting to drive erratically. Hopefully, their own self-awareness would make them realize they themselves are driving poorly, such as perhaps starting to fall asleep after having been driving for hours on end. If you had a passenger in the car, they might be able to alert the driver if the driver is starting to do something amiss. This is exactly what the Self-Aware

AI element tries to do, it becomes the overseer of the AI, and tries to detect when the AI has become faulty or confused, and then find ways to overcome the issue.

D-13: Economic

The economic aspects of a self-driving car are not per se a technology aspect of a self-driving car, but the economics do indeed impact the nature of a self-driving car. For example, the cost of outfitting a self-driving car with every kind of possible sensory device is prohibitive, and so choices need to be made about which devices are used. And, for those sensory devices chosen, whether they would have a full set of features or a more limited set of features.

We are going to have self-driving cars that are at the low-end of a consumer cost point, and others at the high-end of a consumer cost point. You cannot expect that the self-driving car at the low-end is going to be as robust as the one at the high-end. I realize that many of the self-driving car pundits are acting as though all self-driving cars will be the same, but they won't be. Just like anything else, we are going to have self-driving cars that have a range of capabilities. Some will be better than others. Some will be safer than others. This is the way of the real-world, and so we need to be thinking about the economics aspects when considering the nature of self-driving cars.

D-14: Societal

This component encompasses the societal aspects of AI which also impacts the technology of self-driving cars. For example, the famous Trolley Problem involves what choices should a self-driving car make when faced with life-and-death matters. If the self-driving car is about to either hit a child standing in the roadway, or instead ram into a tree at the side of the road and possibly kill the humans in the self-driving car, which choice should be made?

We need to keep in mind the societal aspects will underlie the AI of the self-driving car. Whether we are aware of it explicitly or not, the AI will have embedded into it various societal assumptions.

D-15: Innovation

I included the notion of innovation into the framework because we can anticipate that whatever a self-driving car consists of, it will continue to be innovated over time. The self-driving cars coming out in the next several years will undoubtedly be different and less innovative than the versions that come out in ten years hence, and so on.

Framework Overall

For those of you that want to learn about self-driving cars, you can potentially pick a particular element and become specialized in that aspect. Some engineers are focusing on the sensory devices. Some engineers focus on the controls activation. And so on. There are specialties in each of the elements.

Researchers are likewise specializing in various aspects. For example, there are researchers that are using Deep Learning to see how best it can be used for sensor fusion. There are other researchers that are using Deep Learning to derive good System Action Plans. Some are studying how to develop AI for the Strategic aspects of the driving task, while others are focused on the Tactical aspects.

A well-prepared all-around software developer that is involved in self-driving cars should be familiar with all of the elements, at least to the degree that they know what each element does. This is important since whatever piece of the pie that the software developer works on, they need to be knowledgeable about what the other elements are doing.

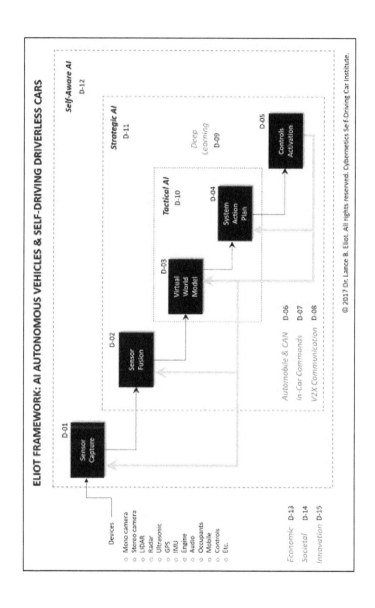

ELIOT FRAMEWORK: AI AUTONOMOUS VEHICLES & SELF-DRIVING DRIVERLESS CARS

CHAPTER 2
LEAVING A TIP
AND
AI SELF-DRIVING CARS

CHAPTER 2

LEAVING A TIP
AND AI SELF-DRIVING CARS

Are you the type of person that never leaves a tip or the kind that nearly always leaves a tip?

Interestingly, Americans spend about $36.4 billion annually on tips so obviously, somebody is opting to put that extra gratuity onto their bill.

It seems like a foregone conclusion that we tend to leave a tip on our restaurant bill, doing so based on the service provided by the waiter or waitress and also perhaps out of a sense of duty or guilt (plus, it could be a mixture of fearful embarrassment or even dreading possible retribution if caught not providing a tip).

Shift your attention away from restaurant tipping and consider tipping in a different context.

Do you tip your vaunted Uber or Lyft ridesharing driver?

On the one hand, it seems like a stretch to suggest that a ridesharing driver should receive a tip since they are merely steering a car from point A to point B, but at the same time you have to admit that Uber or Lyft drivers can choose to do a better or extraordinary job of driving you to your destination, thus warranting a tip for those that are stellar performers.

Some drivers especially aim to please.

They will play music from the radio that fits your tastes. They will offer you free bottled water. They will ask you if the temperature is okay and adjust the settings as needed. They will gently inquire you about your day and be sympathetic when you carp about how rough work is. For a variety of assorted reasons, perhaps providing a tip makes sense.

Tipping for a taxi or cab driver used to be somewhat arduous since you tended to pay for those rides via cash. Having the added dough to cover a tip was at times a tortuous affair, forcing you to dig deeply into your cluttered wallet or purse, plus the mental contortions involved in calculating a suitable tip were painful.

Nowadays, most ridesharing apps offer a suggested tip that can be paid easily, or it can at least calculate a tip based on your instructions. The payment of the tip is seamless and comes directly from your ridesharing account or is charged to your on-file credit card.

One might say that it is nearly friction-free to leave a tip for your ridesharing driver.

If that seems like a suggestion that we are therefore generously giving out ridesharing driver tips, a recent study of Uber riders tends to indicate that we are not doing so as much as you might assume.

Approximately 60% of Uber riders never tip, per the study results, and only a meager 1% always provide a tip.

There are several limitations to the research study, so be cautious in over-generalizing those stats. Nonetheless, it is one of the most comprehensive ridesharing tips-related dataset analyses done to-date.

You might have a sunnier outlook and consider the other side of the coin, namely that apparently 40% of Uber riders do tip from time-to-time.

That's kind of cheerful for those that believe those hard-working Uber drivers deserve a tip.

Of course, interpreting these stats is somewhat problematic due to the aspect that we don't know how often the ridesharing drivers were doing something to warrant a tip.

In other words, if your ridesharing driver picks you up and does nothing out of the ordinary other than driving you to your destination, most would probably say that's an expected aspect of the ridesharing service and there's no basis for therefore providing a tip.

Imagine that 90% of ridesharing rides were not especially memorable and you could then equally imagine that we might only be tipping the 10% of the rides that were memorable.

There is presumably a symbiosis of the driver and rider "duality" that comes to play in the tip preponderance equation.

Another facet might be the ratings systems that ridesharing services use.

Since you get to rate your driver, there are many riders that might consider giving out a high rating as the equivalent of paying a driver a monetary tip. When you give your driver 5 stars, you can justify in your mind that you've effectively given them a tip, whereas you might have given the driver a 4-star rating as a standard score that reflects unexemplary driving.

Here's an interesting question to consider: *Will we give out tips when ridesharing is being performed by true self-driving cars?*

Your first thought might be that it makes absolutely no sense whatsoever to give a tip to a self-driving car.

A true self-driving car is being driven by an AI system, and there's no human driver, so it seems crazy to suggest you'd leave a tip for a disembodied piece of Artificial Intelligence.

Well, you might indeed leave a tip, doing so for reasons that are perhaps not immediately obvious and yet will resonate with your sense of fair play when presented with them.

Let's unpack the matter.

The Levels Of Self-Driving Cars

It is important to clarify what I mean when referring to true self-driving cars.

True self-driving cars are ones that the AI drives the car entirely on its own and there isn't any human assistance during the driving task.

These driverless cars are considered a Level 4 and Level 5, while a car that requires a human driver to co-share the driving effort is usually considered at a Level 2 or Level 3. The cars that co-share the driving task are described as being semi-autonomous, and typically contain a variety of automated add-ons that are referred to as ADAS (Advanced Driver-Assistance Systems).

There is not yet a true self-driving car at Level 5, which we don't yet even know if this will be possible to achieve, and nor how long it will take to get there.

Meanwhile, the Level 4 efforts are gradually trying to get some traction by undergoing very narrow and selective public roadway trials, though there is controversy over whether this testing should be allowed per se (we are all life-or-death guinea pigs in an experiment taking place on our highways and byways, some point out).

Since the semi-autonomous cars require a human driver, such cars aren't particularly going to alter the dynamics of whether to tip your ridesharing driver or not. There is essentially no difference between using a Level 2 or Level 3 versus a conventional car when it comes to driving and therefore doesn't merit any notable changes in your decision about tipping.

Presumably, if you tip your ridesharing driver nowadays, you'll continue to do so in the future. And, those of you that don't tip your ridesharing driver is not going to suddenly start doing so simply because the car is a Level 2 or Level 3.

It is notable to point out that in spite of those idiots that keep posting videos of themselves falling asleep at the wheel of a Level 2 or Level 3 car, do not be misled into believing that you can take away your attention from the driving task while driving a semi-autonomous car.

You are the responsible party for the driving actions of the car, regardless of how much automation might be tossed into a Level 2 or Level 3.

Reasons To Tip A Self-Driving Car

For Level 4 and Level 5 cars, there presumably won't be a human driver at the wheel.

It seems straightforward that if there isn't a human driver you, therefore, won't provide a tip.

Not so fast!

Let's consider a variety of situations that might inspire you to leave a tip:

- **Back-up Safety Driver.** Most of today's tryouts of Level 4 self-driving cars include a human back-up or safety driver that is monitoring the AI system and intended to take over the driving if needed. If you snag a ride in one of these tryout journeys, you might be tempted to leave a tip for your mindful back-up driver. This tends to occur if the person answers your questions during the drive, which many passengers often pepper the driver with what a self-driving car is, how does it work, etc.

- **Remote Teleoperator.** Some self-driving cars are being equipped to allow a remote human driver to take over the car, though I've questioned the practicality of such an arrangement (see my posting here). It's more likely that the remote operator will be the equivalent of an OnStar agent, being able to answer questions or summon emergency services for you. In that case, you might provide a tip to those human remote operators, if they do an outstanding job.

- **Car Cleaner.** When you stay at a hotel, some believe that at the end of your stay that you should leave a tip for the maid or cleaning service, even though you might have never actually seen the person(s) that cleaned your room. When you get into a self-driving car, the odds are that most ridesharing services are going to keep their cars relatively clean, otherwise, riders won't want to use them. If you think the car on an occasion is especially squeaky clean, maybe leave a tip for the cleaning crew.

- **Ride-a-long Nanny.** One open question about letting your kids ride alone in a self-driving car is whether there ought to be an adult supervising them (there won't be a human driver anymore and thus no in-car adult presence). I've predicted that we'll see the rise of a new type of job, the self-driving car nanny or equivalent. Some ridesharing services might provide a screened "nanny" that will accompany the self-driving car ride. Perhaps you'll provide a tip to the in-car adult if your kids report that the person did a great job overseeing them (does that include letting them off-the-hook on finishing their homework during the ride?).

- **Assistance Getting In/Out.** There is supposed to be a mobility-for-all phenomena that will arise due to the advent of driverless cars. People that today are mobility marginalized will finally be able to make use of cars. For some of those people, the act of getting into and out of a car is a chore or arduous difficulty. We are likely to have people that will aid you in getting into and out of a self-driving car, for which you might want to tip those helpful assistants.

- **Small Business Owners.** Pundits predict that self-driving cars will be owned solely by large companies that will have massive fleets of driverless vehicles. I am a bit of a contrarian and claim that we'll still have individuals owning such cars, doing so for their own personal use and to make money by putting the self-driving car onto a ridesharing network while they are at work. You might get into a driverless car that has a sign in it telling you that it is owned by your neighbor down the street, in which case you might be tempted to provide a tip.

- **Anthropomorphic AI.** Humans oftentimes will anthropomorphize inanimate objects, such as the famous Wilson volleyball in the movie *Castaway*. An AI system is going to readily be anthropomorphized since it will be able to converse with riders and seemingly be human-like in its conversation. I'm betting that there will be riders that perceive the AI to be a human and therefore seek to provide a tip to the AI system itself. Guess we'll need a tip jar next to the speakers and a means for the AI to know that you've left some extra coinage for it.

- **AI Developers.** Not all self-driving cars will drive in precisely the same way. It is a myth that driverless cars will strictly drive in a legal manner always and not vary from each other. The driving act involves a lot of latitude. If you get into a self-driving car and it offers a special capability such as a willingness to rush through traffic to get you to work on-time, perhaps you'll be tempted to tip the AI developers that crafted the capability. Of course, AI developers are already a hot commodity and it's doubtful they need such tips, though I'm sure they would gladly accept the added change.

Those are some of the key reasons that might spur riders of driverless cars into providing a tip.

Conclusion

In a Utopian world, we would magically have all self-driving cars and no human-driven cars.

The reality is that we are going to have a mixture of human-driven cars and driverless cars for quite a while.

Initially, there will only be a few self-driving cars on the roads. Gradually, slowly, the mix of driverless cars will rise, and the number of human-driven cars will lessen. Keep in mind that today there are over 250 million conventional cars in the United States and those vehicles aren't going to overnight be replaced with driverless cars.

I point this out to emphasize that for ridesharing purposes you'll be able to choose whether to have your ride be a human-driven car or be a driverless car.

Some are worried that the tips for human drivers will go down precipitously due to the "smoother" ride that you'll get from a driverless car. Plus, the AI system will shut-up when you tell it to do so, and you don't need to deal with the emotional state of the driver.

An equally compelling argument can be made that the human drivers will start getting more tips and more frequently be granted tips by grateful riders. There will be passengers that find the driverless cars to be barren of humanness and therefore seek out the interaction possible with a human driver at the wheel. Tips might go through the roof as such riders opt to reward the human drivers for continuing to drive a car in the face of the robot takeover revolution.

One colleague of mine insists that tipping any ridesharing driver is ridiculous and declares that whether a human is involved or not, and whether the AI is wonderous or not, you'll see a tip over his dead body.

Even the best self-driving car is seemingly unlikely to get a tip out of someone with that viewpoint.

I wonder though if such no-tippers realize that once AI rules the world, those AI systems might seek revenge against those that resisted, and probably put at the top of the list the humans that failed to tip their driverless car.

CHAPTER 3
DIGITAL NUDGING
AND
AI SELF-DRIVING CARS

CHAPTER 3

DIGITAL NUDGING
AND
AI SELF-DRIVING CARS

When you use a ridesharing service such as Uber or Lyft, you usually provide your desired destination when you request a ride. Once your ride arrives, you jump into the car and are whisked away, presumably heading to your designated endpoint.

You can choose to alter your destination location during the driving journey, perhaps doing so because you realized that you had inadvertently specified the wrong address and opt to midcourse correct it.

As a tourist, you might even discuss your destination with the driver, and it could be that the driver might advise you against going to that specific location. The driver might know some local aspects that you are unaware of. Perhaps it's a store that won't open until later in the day, or maybe it's a theme park that if you went to a different one it would be less crowded.

The driver might be offering such local wisdom as a genuine means of helping you and seeking to make your journey a pleasant one.

Of course, the driver might also have other incentives to alter your mind about where to go.

In some places, the driver might be getting a commission by guiding tourists to a certain store or restaurant. Under the guise of merely trying to steer you toward something better than what you had originally indicated as your destination, there might be a kickback or other benefit for the driver to sway you.

Believe it or not, the notion of swaying you in making a choice is often done when you go online to make a purchase; it's called digital nudging.

Suppose you use a web site to figure out which toaster oven to buy. While at the web site, the system displays two models, one that is pricey and looks ugly, and another one that is lower priced and looks slick. You click on the lower-priced one and merrily proceed to purchase it.

It could be that you just fell victim to the classic *decoy technique* of digital nudging.

In the decoy technique, the system purposely puts a lousy choice next to the choice that it really wants you to choose. In your mind, you fall for the notion that there are only two choices and that one of the choices is obviously worse than the other. You might have originally been assuming that you'd look at say ten different models to find the one that is best, but the system has cleverly short-circuited that idea and instead gotten you to narrowly select between a forced dichotomy of a good choice and a bad choice.

I'll combine the digital nudging phenomena with the aspect of choosing your destination when using a ridesharing service.

You get into a ridesharing car and have indicated you want to go to a downtown area bar. The driver chats with you and explains that the bar you've selected is a dud and instead there's a "happening" bar on the other side of town that would be a lot more exciting for you to visit. Thanking the driver profusely, you change the destination to the presumed better bar.

It could be that the driver is right and the bar you've been swayed toward is the better choice. Or, it could be that the driver has other incentives to get you to go to that bar, maybe the owner of the bar gives those recommending drivers free drinks, or perhaps the bar is a further driving distance away and therefore the driver will get paid more for the higher mileage driving journey.

Here's an interesting question: *With true self-driving cars, will you always be taken to whatever destination you've indicated, or might the AI system attempt to digitally nudge you to go to a different endpoint?*

Most people assume that the AI system that's driving the self-driving car will strictly do whatever you've specified and be completely obedient.

Yes, there are some automakers and tech firms that are right now focusing on having the rider indicate a destination and that's all that the passenger needs to do. Come heck or high water, once you get into the vehicle, it's going to do whatever it can to drive to that endpoint.

It's often crudely done right now, such that some of those driverless car tryouts won't let you change your desired destination once you get into the self-driving car and get underway.

In fact, I know some AI developers that say that if a person originally indicates a destination X, the driverless car should go to destination X, doing so with no variations allowed. When pointed out to the AI coder that the person might change their mind midway, these dogmatic AI developers insist that people shouldn't be so stupid about where they want to go, and they are going to be stuck with going to where they originally stipulated to go. Tough luck otherwise.

I've repeatedly exhorted that there's a lot more involved in taking a driving journey than just specifying upfront the desired destination. In the real-world, riders frequently decide during a driving journey to make short stops or swing through an interim waypoint (I'm hungry, a passenger might say to a driver, please use that nearby drive-thru burger place to get me a combo meal).

There is going to be a great deal of exasperation and frustration with the use of self-driving cars if the public is going to be treated to such a simpleton approach to driving that you can only go from point A to point B, doing so without any kind of malleability of your driving journey midcourse.

If the AI developers eventually make their driving journey components savvier, not only will the AI driving system be able to adjust to your driving destination changes, it could take this pliability one step further and try to nudge you.

Do you want an AI system offering nudges to sway your mind about where you are going?

Some think it's a wonderful idea, others are worried that it opens the proverbial Pandora's box.

Let's unpack the matter.

The Levels Of Self-Driving Cars

It is important to clarify what I mean when referring to true self-driving cars.

True self-driving cars are ones that the AI drives the car entirely on its own and there isn't any human assistance during the driving task.

These driverless cars are considered a Level 4 and Level 5, while a car that requires a human driver to co-share the driving effort is usually considered at a Level 2 or Level 3. The cars that co-share the driving task are described as being semi-autonomous, and typically contain a variety of automated add-ons that are referred to as ADAS (Advanced Driver-Assistance Systems).

There is not yet a true self-driving car at Level 5, which we don't yet even know if this will be possible to achieve, and nor how long it will take to get there.

Meanwhile, the Level 4 efforts are gradually trying to get some traction by undergoing very narrow and selective public roadway trials, though there is controversy over whether this testing should be allowed per se (we are all life-or-death guinea pigs in an experiment taking place on our highways and byways, some point out).

Since the semi-autonomous cars require a human driver, such cars aren't particularly going to alter the dynamics of how to choose your destination. There is essentially no difference between using a Level 2 or Level 3 versus a conventional car when it comes to interacting with the driver and therefore doesn't merit any notable changes in your destination decisions.

Presumably, if you at times discuss destination changes with the driver, you'll continue to do so in the future.

It is notable to point out that in spite of those dolts that keep posting videos of themselves falling asleep at the wheel of a Level 2 or Level 3 car, do not be misled into believing that you can take away your attention from the driving task while driving a semi-autonomous car.

You are the responsible party for the driving actions of the car, regardless of how much automation might be tossed into a Level 2 or Level 3.

True Self-Driving Cars And Destinations

For the use of Level 4 and Level 5 driverless cars, one of the most frequently asked questions about those autonomous vehicles is whether they might opt to take you to a place that you didn't specify, akin to a Frankenstein monster gone amuck.

We ought to first agree that a human driver could certainly decide to take you a different destination than the one that you thought you were going to. In that sense, yes, a self-driving car could likewise opt to take you to a destination that's not of your choosing.

If a human driver takes you adrift, you might not know that they are heading the wrong way, depending upon whether you happen to know the area or perhaps are looking at your smartphone GPS tracking. The same could be said about a driverless car.

Just as with a human driver, there's a chance that the driver has gone askew and wants to take you someplace that you don't necessarily want to go. A human driver or even an AI driving system could opt to kidnap you. These are all possibilities; of which we live today day-to-day with the chances that a human driver might act in an untoward manner.

One argument about the awry human driver is that you could presumably at least try to stop the driver from going to the wrong destination. You might attempt to discuss the matter with the driver or escalate by trying to grab the driver and stop the car.

For self-driving cars, you could interact with the AI system via its Natural Language Processing (NLP) capability, kind of like interacting with an Alexa or Siri and attempt to find out why you aren't going where you specified. The NLP might be simplistic and beguiling to try and discuss such matters, or the AI system might stubbornly seem to be unable to realize your distress about the destination.

As such, many of the automakers and tech firms are putting in place a remote human operator aspect that's like an OnStar. If you are concerned that the AI driving system isn't doing what it is supposed to do, you could invoke the in-car OnStar-like remote connection and discuss the issue with a human operator.

In theory, the human operator might be able to take over the driving task, though I've repeatedly forewarned that allowing remote operation of a driverless car is a bad idea. More likely would be that the remote operator could relay new instructions to the AI onboard system, getting it to realize there is a different destination intended, and then let the AI itself drive the car to the desired destination (rather than the human operator doing so via remote controls).

Of course, one downside of the AI driving system is that you cannot grab it by the shirt collar and attempt to physically override what it is doing. Though you can obviously try to manhandle a human driver (or make that person-handle), the odds of something adverse occurring would seem to be quite high. While scuffling with the driver, the driver might lose complete control of the car and the result is that you and the driver could end up in a deadly car crash.

I'm not saying that a car crash is necessarily worse than if the driver is taking you to an untoward destination, and only pointing out that physically having an altercation with a human driver amid the driving act has its own innate risks.

In a driverless car, there's not much physically you could do to overpower the AI. There are some pundits that believe there should be a governmental mandated "kill switch" included in all driverless cars. This is a topic I'll be covering a future column since it notably has both pluses and minuses as a strategy to cope with these matters.

You could try to find where the computer processors are hidden inside the self-driving car and somehow rip them out or otherwise bash them into oblivion (well, yes and no, since you need to keep in mind that those on-board electronics are going to be generally well-protected and it won't be easy to get access to them while the car is in motion).

Destroying the AI system though has a similar downside to roughing up a human driver. For a truly self-driving car, once the computers are out of commission, the car while in-motion can become an unguided missile or might come to a stop or halt in an undesirable manner.

You might be wondering: *Why would the AI system anyway be trying to take you to a destination that's not of your choosing?*

There are several reasons, some benign, others that are worrisome.

One benign reason for a destination that's not where you wanted to go could be due to the self-driving car being set up as a kind of shuttle or bus-like service. Perhaps the driverless car you got into was programmed to drive around town and stop at six pre-specified places. Or, maybe it is being used in a retirement community and only goes to the main townhouse and to several on-property bus-like stops.

Perhaps you hastily got into the self-driving car and assumed that you could tell it where you wanted to go. If indeed the driverless car is on a pre-determined mission, the odds are that you are now going along for a ride.

There is the potential for nefarious reasons that a destination might be off-putting.

Suppose a hacker managed to electronically send a remote command to the driverless car, instructing the AI to go to a destination that differs from what you specified. This possibility showcases the dual-edged sword of allowing a remote operator to tingle with the AI system. In some instances, it might be a bona fide remote operator authorized to do so, though this also then opens the door toward a bad hat actor trying to do the same.

Consider The Nudges

So far, the discussion been about the AI driving the self-driving car to a destination that you didn't choose.

Time to revisit the earlier points about digital nudges.

Suppose the AI opts to sway you into choosing a destination that you didn't originally have in mind, which might be a good nudge or a sour nudge.

There is the possibility that the AI could be genuinely aiming to help you out, and perhaps the AI developers realized there are going to be occasions when riders choose an inappropriate location.

For example, you specify an abandoned and boarded-up hotel, not realizing that the hotel went out of business, and thus the AI perhaps informs you that you would be wise to select a different hotel.

You then do a quick online search and find a viable hotel, relaying the address to the AI system of the driverless car, or maybe just verbally telling the AI to take you to the new destination.

Notice that you are the one specifying the destination.

Another variant could be that the AI offers an alternative hotel, after first letting you know that the originally proffered hotel is closed-up. You then agree to the new hotel, and the AI proceeds to the newly agreed destination.

Once again, you are essentially specifying the destination, in this case, based on the AI's recommendation.

These examples then are unlike the earlier circumstance of the AI choosing a destination that you were not involved in selecting.

The nudging by the AI might be for other less altruistic reasons.

Imagine that the owner of the self-driving car that you are using on a ridesharing journey has made a backroom deal with a large chain grocery store.

When you perchance get into the driverless car, and if you specify a different grocery store that's nearby the large chain version, the AI might coyly let you know that the large chain store is having a half-off sale today.

Upon being told about the half-off deal, you quickly tell the AI to switch to the large chain store as the desired destination.

Maybe the half-off deal is better for you, or maybe not.

Meanwhile, the owner of the driverless car has maybe just pocketed a little extra dough for having sway a rider to the large chain store.

Conclusion

Many assume that driverless cars will be a neutral form of transport and merely take people from point A to point B.

That's a naïve perspective.

Sure, right now, the focus is entirely on being able to get a self-driving car to properly navigate the roads and be safe in doing so.

Once we get past the initial aspects of having driverless cars that work appropriately, there is no question that the driving efforts will further be monetized.

Fleet owners of self-driving cars are going to seek ways to wring more dollars out of their expensive driverless cars. There are in-car advertising possibilities, along with the driverless car acting as a roving billboard.

Another facet of making money would be to allow for the digital nudging of passengers, getting those riders to be mind-tricked into going to where there's more money to be made by the owner.

Don't assume that I am saying that this kind of driverless car induced greed is inherently bad or wrong since it could be that the outcome is better for the rider too.

My point is that we need to be awakened to the notion that where a self-driving car will take you is not a foregone conclusion and we'll all need to be on our toes about going along for a ride.

CHAPTER 4

CARPOOL LANES
AND
AI SELF-DRIVING CARS

CHAPTER 4

CARPOOL LANES AND
AI SELF-DRIVING CARS

Carpool lanes are undeniably both beloved and hated.

For those drivers that can utilize a carpool lane, they relish the fact that much of the time the carpool lane has fewer cars in it and therefore moves at a faster pace than the rest of the traffic (the so-called mixed lanes).

Meanwhile, drivers stuck in the bumper-to-bumper mixed lanes are at times irked to see the free-flowing cars in the carpool lane.

What makes them so special?

Who do they think they are?

Oftentimes, renegade drivers in the mixed lanes will try to sneak into a carpool lane, even though they legally aren't supposed to be in there. The mindset seems to be that if you jump quickly into the carpool lane, zip ahead at light speed, and then leap back out of the special lane, the odds of getting caught are slim.

During my morning commute, I see law-breaking drivers commit such a crime all the time.

This makes the law-abiding drivers in the mixed lanes become infuriated at the carpool lanes, namely that the carpool lanes can so easily be "stolen" by other drivers and do so without any direct repercussions.

Overall, most people are sympathetic with the intent of carpool lanes as a set aside to have society shape what kinds of cars we drive and how many people we carry, but when those scofflaw drivers that aren't supposed to use the carpool lanes get away with their untoward incursions, we become enraged at the loathsome drivers and the very existence of the carpool lanes that permit such lawlessness.

If you want to enumerate the downsides of carpool lanes, you can also include the aspect that getting into and out of carpool lanes is known to be a producer of car accidents.

Here's what happens.

A carpool lane is moving at top speed, while the traffic in the next lane over is moving sluggishly. A driver that misjudges getting into the carpool lane, assuming they legally can do so, merges into the special lane at a snail-like speed. Bang, a carpool car and the merging car bash into each other.

Likewise, when a car exits from the carpool lane, they often do so at a high speed, and inadvertently ram into slower traffic in an adjacent lane.

You could try to argue that those slipshod drivers are careless and therefore it's a human driving problem, though similarly, you could say that the fundamental design of carpool lanes lends itself to putting drivers into situations that lead to car crashes. Roadway infrastructure that tempts drivers into making mistakes is poorly designed and indefensible.

Adding fuel to the fire, you've got interlopers that break the rules entirely and try to enter into the carpool lane when they aren't supposed to do so or try to exit from the carpool lane when it isn't allowed.

One must ask, do carpool lanes actually work?

In some locales, there is an argument to be made that the enormous cost for a carpool lane is marginally worth the benefits it accrues.

To enact a carpool lane, you either need to take an entire lane out of normal service and dedicate it to this special purpose, or you need to expand the roadway to accommodate an additional lane to serve as a carpool lane. Adding lanes to an existing highway or freeway is a multi-millions of dollars proposition (sometimes billions of dollars), and the construction process will likely disrupt existing traffic for an extended period.

Some would vehemently argue that by not allowing mixed traffic into that dedicated lane, you are making the mixed traffic situation worse.

A counter-argument is that if those drivers are upset about sitting in the mixed traffic lanes, those drivers ought to look in the mirror and realize they need to change their type of car or include more passengers so that they too could enjoy the pleasures of a carpool lane.

Round and round you can go on the never-ending debate about the merits of carpool lanes. The battle between those in favor of a carpool lane versus those opposed can be loud and quite acrimonious.

This brings up an interesting question: *With the advent of true self-driving cars, will we continue to have carpool lanes or will be done away with the vaunted and controversial special lanes?*

Let's unpack the matter.

The Levels Of Self-Driving Cars

It is important to clarify what I mean when referring to true self-driving cars.

True self-driving cars are ones that the AI drives the car entirely on its own and there isn't any human assistance during the driving task.

These driverless cars are considered a Level 4 and Level 5, while a car that requires a human driver to co-share the driving effort is usually considered at a Level 2 or Level 3. The cars that co-share the driving task are described as being semi-autonomous, and typically contain a variety of automated add-ons that are referred to as ADAS (Advanced Driver-Assistance Systems).

There is not yet a true self-driving car at Level 5, which we don't yet even know if this will be possible to achieve, and nor how long it will take to get there.

Meanwhile, the Level 4 efforts are gradually trying to get some traction by undergoing very narrow and selective public roadway trials, though there is controversy over whether this testing should be allowed per se (we are all life-or-death guinea pigs in an experiment taking place on our highways and byways, some point out).

Since semi-autonomous cars require a human driver, such cars aren't particularly going to make a difference in our use of carpool lanes. There is a minor argument to be made that perhaps the Level 2 and Level 3 features will aid in forewarning the human driver when merging poorly into or out of a carpool lane, but the human driver is still the judge and jury in deciding what action to take.

In fact, it is notable to point out that in spite of those drivers that keep posting videos of themselves falling asleep at the wheel of a Level 2 or Level 3 car, do not be misled into believing that you can take away your attention from the driving task while driving a semi-autonomous car.

You are the responsible party for the driving actions of the car, regardless of how much automation might be tossed into a Level 2 or Level 3.

Self-Driving Cars And Carpool Lanes

For Level 4 and Level 5 true self-driving cars, we might be able to reconsider the notion and use of carpool lanes.

First, let's tackle the conventional reasons for wanting to have carpool lanes.

Most carpool lanes today are set up to allow EV (Electrical Vehicles) as an immediate use for the carpool lane.

If you are driving an EV, you are typically allowed to proceed to use the carpool lane, regardless of whether you had obtained any prior tags or permission to do so and regardless of how many passengers you have in the car. The idea is that society wants to cut down on gasoline-powered car emissions, and so by giving EVs a free pass to use the carpool lane, it will incentivize people to switch to EV's.

Well, fortunately, the odds are that true self-driving cars are going to be EV's.

Part of the reason for the EV use of self-driving cars is that computers and sensors require a lot of electrical energy. Sure, a gasoline-powered car could potentially generate the needed power, but an EV is ready-made to do so.

Furthermore, most of the self-driving car makers are aiming to dovetail into the presumed societal shift toward EV's. It would seem rather short-sighted to instead be putting your eggs into a gasoline-powered car that would receive consternation by energy-conscious people and get dinged for being bad for the environment.

A lousy way to try and get traction for true self-driving cars.

If we had a world of all true self-driving cars, and they were EV's, this facet would knock out one of the pillars for needing to have carpool lanes.

Consider another reason for today's carpool lanes, specifically the act of carpooling.

Society hopes to get more people per car and avoid the seeming irresistible act of having solo drivers in cars. By providing today's carpool lanes, it encourages drivers to find others to travel with them.

If you have more people per car, the belief is that you'll have fewer cars on the roadways, freeing up congestion.

True self-driving cars won't require and will not have a human driver.

When you take a trip in a self-driving car, all the occupants will be passengers. Some hope that this will spur people to truly carpool, especially since the interior of driverless cars will be more spacious (since you can remove the human-used driving controls that take-up space).

As I've elaborated in one of my other pieces, we don't yet know whether self-driving cars will promote carpooling or whether it might simply bring us more solo occupancy riding.

In theory, if you are in the camp that says self-driving cars will encourage carpooling, this is yet another takedown of a pillar for needing carpool lanes.

Perhaps people will carpool in self-driving cars just because of the nature of self-driving cars, and no longer need any added incentive such as a special travel lane. You could also argue that since there aren't any drivers in the driverless car, those in the driverless car might not even realize whether the traffic is congested or not. The attention inside the self-driving car might be on interacting with other passengers or watching a streaming movie.

Keeping count, we've so far edged out the pollution abating reason for carpool lanes and somewhat undercut the need to force people into carpooling due to the assumption that people will freely do so on their own as a result of driverless cars being available.

Another factor for conventional carpool lanes is traffic management, though this is a contentious topic, for sure.

One argument is that carpool lanes aid in traffic flow.

Such a claim raises eyebrows since the traffic overall would presumably flow more smoothly if all cars could use all lanes, rather than having a small subset of cars use a lane that others aren't able to use.

For true self-driving cars, they will be outfitted with V2V (vehicle-to-vehicle) electronic communications, allowing nearby driverless cars to digitally communicate with each other. In addition, self-driving cars are going to have V2I (vehicle-to-infrastructure) electronic communications, enabling the roadway traffic lights and other elements to communicate with driverless cars.

Some believe that if properly managed, self-driving cars will "talk" with each other about the flow of traffic. Hey, there's debris in the second lane up ahead, so everybody moves gently over to avoid the problem.

This kind of communication could significantly reduce traffic delays and disruptions.

With the combined punch of both V2V and V2I, traffic might flow more smoothly via self-driving cars, doing so as a result of the coordination and cooperation among the driverless vehicles.

Today's human drivers are living in a dog-eat-dog world of tussles with other drivers for every inch of roadway travel. To some extent, this human greed in driving is what hampers traffic flow, though there is surprisingly a good side (sometimes) to this mankind-derived style of driving (see my post here).

Conclusion

The case seems to have been made that we can dispense with carpool lanes once self-driving cars have arrived.

Not so fast!

One issue to consider is that we are going to have a mixture of human-driven cars and self-driving cars for many years to come.

There are about 250 million conventional cars in the United States alone. Those everyday cars are not going to suddenly become driverless cars. Self-driving cars will gradually emerge and at first, be a tiny proportion of the cars on our roadways. Over many years, likely decades, we'll gradually see a shift toward less and less conventional cars and more so driverless cars on our streets.

During that interim period of a heavy mix of human-driven cars, maybe we should keep the carpool lanes in place.

You could add a rule to the carpool lane access rights that may be all driverless cars can use it too, in addition to those that are driving EV's or those that have two or more passengers.

If society wants to encourage people to use driverless cars, the carpool lanes might eventually be dedicated exclusively to driverless car use only.

As a side note, please don't confuse the point about making carpool lanes into lanes for driverless cars with a different topic that has some controversy associated with it. Namely, there are some that believe that the only means to ensure the safety of self-driving cars is to put them into their own separate lanes.

Maybe we could reduce the difficulties of the AI having to deal with human-driven cars by setting aside roads or lanes that only driverless cars could use. Without those pesky human drivers in the same lane, it would make life easier for the AI.

I don't subscribe to that notion.

It's my fervent belief that we need to make sure that the AI can handle driving near to and among human drivers. Only in very narrow circumstances might it be sensible to set aside special roads or lanes, but overall any properly done and true self-driving car should not need to be shielded away from the realities of driving on our public streets.

One last point about carpool lanes is an aspect that becomes feasible in an era of true self-driving cars.

Since driverless cars have the V2V and V2I electronic means to communicate with each other, you could pretty much establish a kind of virtual carpool lane.

Here's how that might work.

A slew of driverless cars is on the freeway. Traffic is moving at a constant flow but a somewhat slower pace than the freeway itself could allow.

Within one of the driverless cars, a pregnant woman is about to give birth. The AI in her car communicates with other nearby self-driving cars and explains that this woman needs to be rushed to the nearest hospital.

The self-driving cars all begin to open up a path for the driverless car with the pregnant woman. Maybe all of the self-driving cars move out of the fast lane and let this one driverless car zip along in it, free of any other cars in the way.

Or, maybe the driverless car weaves in and out of the other cars on the freeway, doing so like a football player that's scampering down the field. In this case, all the other cars are purposely opening up spaces between them to allow for the one driverless car to readily zoom ahead in traffic.

My point is that we might not need to have a physically dedicated carpool lane anymore. Instead, there would be the possibility of virtual lanes. You might not even refer to this as lanes per se. These are paths through traffic that are jiggered on-the-fly and by the overarching cooperation of the self-driving cars.

Yay!

What a boon to mankind.

Maybe.

We will need to figure out the rules of when such virtual paths can be instantiated.

If you are late for work, does that give you the right to raise a red flag and request that all other driverless cars get out of your way?

Probably not a good enough reason.

All told, we might gradually see the extinction of dedicated and physical carpool lanes.

In their replacement might be on-the-fly virtual paths that can be crafted as needed and when legally allowed, occur via electronic communications among self-driving cars.

Imagine that you are driving on the freeway, one of the few remaining human drivers and all of a sudden all of the driverless cars around you started shifting back-and-forth in their lanes and you have no idea why they are conducting a seemingly intricate ballet.

Those driverless cars might be making room for that self-driving car with a top dignitary, or maybe the AI has decided that you, the human driver in the mix, an oddball among all the self-driving cars, needs to be boxed-in and slowed down.

Serves you right for not giving up your driving privilege and allowing the AI overlords to run our roadways (here's a link for some interesting AI conspiracy theories about the future of driving).

CHAPTER 5

SLEEP SOLVING
AND
AI SELF-DRIVING CARS

CHAPTER 5

SLEEP SOLVING

AND

AI SELF-DRIVING CARS

America is losing sleep over losing sleep.

According to recent studies, nearly one-third of Americans get less than 6 hours of sleep per night.

Believe it or not, the recommended amount of sleep that we ought to be getting is about seven to nine hours a night, though it sure seems like many people don't have that kind of luxury allowed in their frantic daily schedules.

Big deal, you might be mumbling, so what that lots of people aren't getting enough sleep.

In fact, it used to be that cheating on sleep and not getting much snooze time per night was a badge of honor. We were often told that the world's top performers prided themselves on getting a mere four hours of sleep a night. Only lazy people stretched their sleep time to six or more hours.

If you wanted to keep up with the Joneses, you had to stop whining about lack of sleep and just push yourself to the limits.

Taking a nap during the day was verboten and sneakily done by wimps only.

And the motto that was supposed to run our lives was that you'll be able to get plenty of sleep once you're dead, thus no need to waste time now on getting some shuteye.

The consequences of cutting corners on sleep are notably quite alarming.

Records show that people with sleep deficiencies are more prone to getting into accidents. These are accidents of all kinds, including while at the job or even when driving your car to or from work.

People that obtain less than the recommended amount of sleep time are often readily irritable and can launch into unexpected tirades or fights. They can turn their home life into a horror show by taking out their exhaustion on those close to them. Heart conditions are worsened by a lack of needed sleep. Etc.

Importantly, your overall health is put into heightened jeopardy simply due to a sleep undercount.

In recent years, our attitudes about sleep have shifted, moving away from the bravado of avoiding sleep and becoming instead an embracing of getting the right amount of sleep.

You might say we are experiencing a reawakening on the topic of sleep.

There are tons of mobile apps that you can download and use to embolden your sleep tactics and strategies. Online videos exist aplenty that will provide soothing sounds and images, lulling you into a sleepy state. Companies have opted to create special sleep zones in the office area, including stocking darkened rooms with futuristic looking sleep pods.

Of course, some of these efforts to help you get more sleep are at times uttered out of both sides of the mouth.

On the one hand, a company says that you ought to get at least eight hours of sleep per night and can grab a catnap at the office in case you need to do so. But, in the same breath, firms are telling you that you need to be on-the-clock 24x7 via your smartphone, responding to emails and text messages within moments of receiving them.

How can you get any kind of quiet and continuous sleep if you know that at any moment your smartphone will harken you to answer instantly and you need to be seemingly always on-alert and aware of what's happening at work?

Plus, consider the daily drive that you likely undertake for getting to the office each day.

If you live in any major city or work in a bustling locale, the odds are that you need to get up before the sun rises so that you can try to avoid the dreaded traffic on the freeway. At the end of the workday, you perhaps spend another hour or two driving home. All this driving is not only stressful, but it also cuts into the amount of time that you have per day to do other tasks.

When you add up the things that you believe need to be undertaken each day, and when the number is higher than the amount of wakefulness time that you currently have allotted yourself, you typically choose to adjust that which seems easiest to reduce, namely the amount of time you have to sleep.

It's an easy equation and a (seemingly) no-brainer decision.

Do you push back on the other responsibilities and duties, or do you silently cut back on your sleep time?

Nobody will know or need to be convinced about letting you diminish your sleep time. Trying to cut down on your other tasks is much harder, having to negotiate with others and find a means to do less, but the sleep deprivation angle is straightforward and a no-fuss option.

As already mentioned, you'll ultimately pay the price for cutting down on your sleep time, though that's not something readily apparent at first, and anyway, you assume that you can exist on barebones sleep since you are one heck of a rough-and-tough person (there's that bravado again!).

Here's an intriguing question: *Could the advent of true self-driving cars potentially solve America's sleep deprivation problem?*

Let's unpack the matter.

The Levels Of Self-Driving Cars

It is important to clarify what I mean when referring to true self-driving cars.

True self-driving cars are ones that the AI drives the car entirely on its own and there isn't any human assistance during the driving task.

These driverless cars are considered a Level 4 and Level 5, while a car that requires a human driver to co-share the driving effort is usually considered at a Level 2 or Level 3. The cars that co-share the driving task are described as being semi-autonomous, and typically contain a variety of automated add-ons that are referred to as ADAS (Advanced Driver-Assistance Systems).

There is not yet a true self-driving car at Level 5, which we don't yet even know if this will be possible to achieve, and nor how long it will take to get there.

Meanwhile, the Level 4 efforts are gradually trying to get some traction by undergoing very narrow and selective public roadway trials, though there is controversy over whether this testing should be allowed per se (we are all life-or-death guinea pigs in an experiment taking place on our highways and byways, some point out).

Since semi-autonomous cars require a human driver, there is nothing notable about such cars being able to alleviate or mitigate the sleep deprivation problem.

It is crucial to point out that in spite of those human drivers that keep posting videos of themselves falling asleep at the wheel of a Level 2 or Level 3 car, do not be misled into believing that you can take away your attention from the driving task while driving a semi-autonomous car.

You are the responsible party for the driving actions of the car, regardless of how much automation might be tossed into a Level 2 or Level 3.

Self-Driving Cars And Reclaiming Sleep

For Level 4 and Level 5 true self-driving cars, it might be prudent to consider how their adoption could aid in overcoming the sleep deprivation issue.

First, keep in mind that with true autonomous cars there is no need for a human driver. Everyone inside a driverless car is a passenger.

Per nationwide statistics, we are putting in about 70 billion driving hours per year in the United States, all of which would eventually (presumably) get converted into passenger time.

While inside a self-driving car, you'll have additional marvels of technology, including 5G high-speed Internet access. You can play online games to your heart's content. You can watch real-time streaming videos and catch up on those movies or TV shows that you enjoy watching.

During a driving journey, you could interact with others that might be inside your self-driving car, since much of the time these will be ridesharing service driverless cars, or you could use the Internet to connect with colleagues at the office or anywhere around the world.

In short, you could potentially be quite productive while inside a self-driving car.

Or, you could sleep.

That being said, let's agree that sleep can be just as productive as many of those other activities that I've just listed.

If you use an hour of your daily commute time to play an online game versus grabbing a catnap, which of the two approaches to utilizing your time is more productive?

Undoubtedly, for those that are not getting enough sleep at night, the catnap is the winner.

You'll be healthier for taking the nap, less irritable, less prone to mistakes and accidents, and otherwise gain significant advantages that playing an online game would be hard-pressed to equal (unless I suppose, you could win a million dollars while playing your favorite online game).

Remember those mobile apps that I mentioned can be downloaded and used to guide your sleep desiring efforts?

Those same kinds of apps will be readily available while you are in a driverless car. Some ridesharing fleets will undoubtedly encourage the act of sleeping, offering free access to such apps. Furthermore, the interior of the car might be specially prepared for sleeping purposes.

The interior of self-driving cars won't need to use up space for driving controls, those aren't needed when there isn't a human driver involved (the AI has driving controls under-the-hood, so to speak).

As such, the inside of driverless cars will aim to allow people to catch some sleep.

Seats will recline into beds. There might be no seats at all and only beds.

The windows of the driverless car will likely be replaced with LED screens to allow you to watch movies and videos. Those window LED screens could just as well be shut off to make the interior dark. Or, the displays might show calm scenes of pleasant Caribbean beaches, allowing you to escape the fact that your driverless car is jammed in traffic on a busy freeway.

Sleep gurus that today coach you via your smartphone, sending you texts or getting connected in a Skype-like manner, they will be able to beam into your driverless car via Internet access and offer you soothing words of advice about how to do a catnap.

The AI that's driving the car can get into the act of helping you sleep too.

Rather than taking curves and turns in a harsh manner, the AI might employ a human-asleep mode that seeks to drive the car in a smooth and caring manner. No sudden stops. No lurching starts. And, rather than telling you about how the drive is coming along, the AI's Natural Language Processing (NLP), akin to an Alexa or Siri, might be mum and let you enjoy the peace and quiet inside the self-driving car.

When you need to take longer trips, you can get a full night's sleep inside the driverless car. During the day, presumably, you'd only get brief snippets of sleep time.

Some believe that we might end-up living in our driverless cars.

You could use your self-driving car to get to work, then after work take you to a bar or restaurant, and then rather than going home, the driverless car would park someplace, and you'd sleep there overnight.

The facility that you used to park the driverless car overnight might have a shower and maybe even a workout room, and once you've refreshed yourself, onward you go in your self-driving car to work or whatever is your next destination.

I'm not especially convinced about the notion that we'll abandon having homes and be using self-driving cars as a replacement or surrogate for our housing, but I bring up the possibility to appease those that think we will ultimately be living full-time in our driverless cars.

Admittedly, some people might do so, of which there are social aspects that will need to be contended with to figure out how that's going to be feasible and practical. Suppose someone decides to park their driverless car in front of your home in your neighborhood, doing so each night, and they sleep in that self-driving car.

You might be quite displeased with that situation.

Conclusion

Well, it seems like self-driving cars are going to ride to the rescue and finally overcome the sleep deprivation malady.

Not so fast!

We don't yet know whether people will feel trusting enough to sleep while inside a driverless car. If you are nervous that the driverless car is going to do something amiss, there's little chance you could allow your mind to sink into a deep sleep.

You would always be keeping one eye open.

Assuming the public believes that driverless cars are safe, and assuming they are indeed safe, the next consideration is whether people can comfortably sleep inside a moving car.

Some people get car sick while trying to sleep in today's cars. The motion of the car seems to turn its stomach.

Makers of self-driving cars will likely employ all sorts of trickery to try and help people get to sleep, though we don't yet know how many people will nonetheless still get car sick and be unable to get shuteye in a self-driving car.

An even more looming barrier to sleeping inside a driverless car is the perceived "lost opportunity" of using the driving journey time for some other purpose.

You could have played another round of your preferred online game and scored ten thousand points.

You could have watched the latest movie that everyone is talking about.

Work will also likely try to intrude upon your driverless car sleeping time.

Your boss might assert that the time during your daily commute ought to be spent catching up on needed paperwork. Or, you are supposed to schedule and undertake work calls and online conference meetings during the time that you are in your driverless car.

Maybe you are sharing the driverless car with others, and there's little chance to recline your seat into a bed, plus the noise and chatter of the other passengers would be like trying to catch some sleep while on a hectic airplane ride.

Imagine the shame you might endure of showing up at the office and when asked whether you already got your preliminary work done, you instead sheepishly admit that you fell asleep in the driverless car.

Yikes, you lazy bum, you had a high-speed Internet connection and a fully private hour of time, and yet to waste it on sleep!

Shame on you.

Or, should it be shame on the employer for creeping into the only time that you had to make yourself a better work that's more alert and ready for a day's job?

Only time will tell, and we'll have to wait and see if self-driving cars can get us to stop thinking about losing sleep, and instead be happy that we are gaining sleep that was otherwise was being shortchanged.

Sleep on that one!

CHAPTER 6

NOSTRADAMUS AND
AI SELF-DRIVING CARS

CHAPTER 6

NOSTRADAMUS AND AI SELF-DRIVING CARS

Nostradamus.

We all associate Nostradamus as being that soothsayer that was able to seemingly predict the future.

His true name was Michel de Nostredame, and of the many accomplishments he had as both a physician and an astrologer, most know him best via his famous book *Les Propheties*. Published in 1555, the book is a collection of several hundred quatrains.

Quatrains are essentially short poems, consisting of four lines, and have been used since ancient times to tell stories or otherwise convey a message of one kind or another (of course, there is the possibility that a quatrain could be utterly meaningless and merely be a rambling of random words).

In the case of Nostradamus, he apparently intended for us to become aware of his predictions about the future and opted to do so in quatrains. Thus, his book is a purposeful effort.

Within the collection of quatrains, he grouped them into a series of sets that we might call verses and for which he referred to them at the time as "Centuries" (presumably due to each set containing one hundred quatrains).

Most anyone that has seriously studied his quatrains would generally agree that they are often difficult to decipher in terms of what Nostradamus was trying to convey. The quatrains are coated in metaphors, mythological references, astrological concoctions, and pretty much a mystery cloaked in an enigma.

Nonetheless, many would also swear that Nostradamus nailed many global events that have happened since he first published the book in 1555.

Some claim that his prophesies foretold the rise of Hitler. Some believe that he prophesized the 9/11 attacks in the United States. Add to the list the French Revolution, the atomic bombs that were dropped during WWII, the Great Fire of London, and so on.

Today, whenever someone makes an outstretched prediction of the future, we are apt to quickly invoke the legend of Nostradamus as an indicator of being a seer.

How did Nostradamus accomplish this remarkable and enduring feat?

Was he able to divine the future via some other-worldly capacity?

Or, maybe he was a time traveler, having visited the future and then went back to 1555, deciding to write down his "predictions" when he knew for sure they were going to happen.

Perhaps he had a complex calculus, being able to read earthly signs and inspect the stars, and with mathematical precision arrive at his soothsaying.

Well, keep in mind that there are some that don't believe he made any valid predictions at all.

It could be that he just wrote about a bunch of stuff, and we have interpreted his musings as though they were predictions about the future.

Given the ambiguities within his writings, it could be claimed that you can assign any meaning that you want to his quatrains. His quatrains are essentially a type of Rorschach test, and you, the reader, bring to them whatever is embedded already in your mind.

Let's consider one quick example so that you can decide how you feel about his quatrains.

Try this on for size:
The great man will be struck down in the day by a thunderbolt,
An evil deed foretold by the bearer of a petition.
According to the prediction, another falls at night time.
Conflict at Reims, London and a pestilence in Tuscany.

Which significant historical event do you think this quatrain predicts?

Give up?

Some assert that the quatrain clearly and unambiguously predicted the assassination of President John Kennedy and his brother Bobby Kennedy.

Read it again.

In the first line, the "great man" would be John Kennedy, and his assassination is the part that says he will "be struck down in the day."

Recall that JFK was shot by a sniper during daytime (or so the government would have us believe; some might say). Being shot by a bullet from a rifle could be likened to the "thunderbolt" reference in that first line.

Bobby Kennedy was killed at midnight, which is apparently predicted in the third line when it states that "another falls at night time."

Those that believe the quatrain made that specific prediction are often pressed for what the second line and the fourth line mean in the context of those assassinations.

Generally, the "petition" in the second line is construed as prior death threats that were made on their lives, while the fourth line seems to not have any specific meaning that can be reasonably associated with those murderous acts.

Does the aspect that we are only able to directly match two of the lines to the assassinations mean that we can reject the prediction as not being valid?

Not so, many would argue.

It could be that we aren't astute enough to connect the other lines. Or, maybe those other lines are about something still ahead, in our future, and for which we will all later realize that those future events connected back to the assassinations.

One view is that it is all hogwash.

The overly generous interpretations are merely a contorted attempt to find meaning where no such meaning exists.

More politely, in deference to the wisdom and talents of Nostradamus, maybe it is a reference to some entirely different event, and we've botched things and mismatched it.

In any case, I like to play a little game when the quatrains are matched to a real-world event.

Each line of the quatrain is worth either a point score of zero or one.

If there is something within a line that can be "reasonably" construed as tying to a real-world event that is postulated as underlying the prediction, you score a point for that line. It is helpful if there is more than one matching clue in a line, which is reassuring, though the line still only gets a one-point score.

Thus, a quatrain can be scored as a zero if none of the lines seem to match to an identified real-world event. If only one line pertains, the quatrain gets a score of one, etc. If all four lines have each some relevant tie, the quatrain gets a score of four.

We'll add a bonus point for a quatrain that applies to a single cohesive historical event. In other words, it could be that the four lines refer to disparate historical events, which merits a score of four, while if the quatrain in its entirety has its eye on a single overall event then a bonus of one point is allotted.

Okay, we now have a handy scoring system, let's call it the NOstradamus Prediction Estimator (the acronym is NOPE), offering a score of zero to five, with five being the topmost or "best fit" score.

Here's an intriguing question for you: *Did Nostradamus perchance predict the advent of true self-driving cars?*

Say, what?

Impossible, you might howl out.

Let's unpack the matter and see.

The Levels Of Self-Driving Cars

It is important to clarify what I mean when referring to true self-driving cars.

True self-driving cars are ones that the AI drives the car entirely on its own and there isn't any human assistance during the driving task.

These driverless cars are considered a Level 4 and Level 5, while a car that requires a human driver to co-share the driving effort is usually considered at a Level 2 or Level 3. The cars that co-share the driving task are described as being semi-autonomous, and typically contain a variety of automated add-ons that are referred to as ADAS (Advanced Driver-Assistance Systems).

There is not yet a true self-driving car at Level 5, which we don't yet even know if this will be possible to achieve, and nor how long it will take to get there.

Meanwhile, the Level 4 efforts are gradually trying to get some traction by undergoing very narrow and selective public roadway trials, though there is controversy over whether this testing should be allowed per se (we are all life-or-death guinea pigs in an experiment taking place on our highways and byways, some point out).

Since semi-autonomous cars require a human driver, the adoption of those types of cars won't be markedly different than conventional cars.

For semi-autonomous cars, it is important that I mention a disturbing aspect that's been arising, namely that in spite of those human drivers that keep posting videos of themselves falling asleep at the wheel of a Level 2 or Level 3 car, we all need to avoid being misled into believing that the driver can take away their attention from the driving task while driving a semi-autonomous car.

You are the responsible party for the driving actions of the car, regardless of how much automation might be tossed into a Level 2 or Level 3.

Self-Driving Cars And Predicted Reality

For Level 4 and Level 5 true self-driving cars, there won't be a human driver involved in the driving task. The occupants inside a driverless car will all be passengers, and there's no human driver needed or utilized inside the car.

Is there a chance that Nostradamus might have predicted true self-driving cars?

If you believe that he predicted other notable historical events, it certainly seems plausible that he might have seen a future that included driverless cars.

Some might argue that the advent of self-driving cars is not of the same import or magnitude as the other historical events that Nostradamus has presumably predicted. You might be tempted to toss driverless cars into the ho-hum bucket and suggest that it would not merit the attention of the grand soothsayer Nostradamus.

Though it is an arguable point, I don't think we've all yet grasped how significant a change in our world there will be if indeed true self-driving cars are achieved.

Those that anticipate a dramatic change in mobility are prone to suggesting that driverless cars are going to have a significant and ongoing transformation of our lives. It is hard for us to envision what things will be like when you no longer need to be a driver or arrange to get a human driver.

Furthermore, as I've stated numerous times, if we can achieve true self-driving cars, it means that we've made a tremendous amount of progress in formulating AI systems, and the odds are that this AI progress can be applied to many other aspects of our lives in terms of other systems and devices that we daily use.

For those that scoff at the matter, I suppose the main consideration is to provide proof of the pudding.

If none of the hundreds of quatrains appears to apply to the advent of self-driving cars, it would seem to place a nail in the coffin of hope that there might be a Nostradamus prediction about driverless cars.

On the other hand, if we could find a quatrain that seems to apply, maybe it would get us into a mode of thinking that perhaps Nostradamus did see ahead to that day.

I'd like to take a stab at this.

Please consider this quatrain:
In 500 years during which more will take into account,
The one who was the ornament of his era:
Then with a shock great clarity he will give,
Which by this century will bring them great contentment.

Give me a moment to explain how this quatrain might well be a predictor of self-driving cars.

The Prediction Explained

Before I launch into the details, keep in mind that we don't yet have true self-driving cars per se.

Pundits anticipate that the tryouts of Level 4 today will gradually expand and become more commonplace by 2025.

Commonplace though doesn't mean prevalent.

We have more than 250 million conventional cars today in the United States alone, and those aren't going to be overnight dumped and replaced by driverless cars. Over many years, the Level 4 driverless cars will presumably be gradually rolled out, and meanwhile, the conventional cars will become obsolete and junked.

Meanwhile, the Level 5 self-driving car that is today merely a gleam in our eyes, it might be emerging perhaps in the range of 2035 or so.

And, suppose that it takes another decade or two before we would have some overall prevalence of driverless cars on our roadways.

Peg that around the year 2055.

You might argue that it will happen somewhat sooner than 2055, or it might take longer, but if you are willing to take a long-view perspective, it would seem "reasonable" based on what we know today to suggest that a target date of around 2055 for the prevalence of driverless cars seems like a fair assessment.

Strap on your seat belt as we are now ready to tackle the Nostradamus quatrain.

The first line says that something will happen "In 500 years."

His book came out in 1555, so let's add 500 years to the date, and you have the year 2055.

Yes, go ahead and double-check the math.

Whoa, the year 2055, which you might recall is the same as the estimated year of driverless car prevalence.

Coincidence or remarkable prediction by Nostradamus?

So far, we only have one line that might seem connected to the future and self-driving cars.

Let's continue our quest.

The second line refers to the "one who was the ornament of his era."

Today's cars are essential to our everyday lives. But, once we have driverless cars, the old-time human-driven car will no longer be an astonishing or notable aspect.

After the next generation of our children's children get used to self-driving cars, they will likely look back upon human-driven cars as though they were the equivalent of a horse and buggy.

You might be willing therefore to consider today's human-driven cars as simply a type of ornament in comparison to the AI advanced true self-driving cars. Conventional cars from a perspective of future generations might be the ornament of an earlier era.

I'm going to score that this quatrain has at least two points, a point for the first line and a point for the second line.

The third line states that "Then with a shock great clarity he will give."

When people see a driverless car for the first time, such as the Level 4 tryouts, and if the back-up human driver is sitting in the backseat or not in the vehicle at all, those people that witness the self-driving car are usually amazed that a car seems to be driving itself.

It is a shock to see.

Also, as mentioned earlier, society isn't able yet to comprehend how different things will be once we have a prevalence of driverless cars. Having a few tryouts in a handful of locales does not convey the full sense of disruption and transformation that we will all ultimately experience.

In short, once there is a prevalence of driverless cars, which is anticipated by sometime around 2055, we might find ourselves surprised at how much it is changing our lives. We will begin to have greater clarity about the importance of achieving self-driving cars.

I'm going to, therefore, add a point for the third line, since it seems to pertain to the future and self-driving cars amidst the shock and clarity it will bring.

The fourth line discusses the aspect that "by this century" there will be "great contentment" that presumably arises due to whatever the first three lines are trying to tell us.

Clearly, the century being referred to must be the 21st century, since that's the time in which the year 2055 will occur.

By having a prevalence of driverless cars, we will have greater access and freedom of travel. Many anticipate that self-driving cars are going to democratize mobility. Those that today are limited in mobility or are mobility disadvantaged will finally have mobility readily available to them.

All of this will happen in the 21st century, getting substantially underway in the estimated year 2055 and continuing certainly until the end of the century or 2100 (maybe by then we'll be beaming around Star Trek-like rather than using cars).

You could suggest that we will find contentment in this century by having driverless cars that can allow us to roam and be mobile, offering democratization of mobility and the vaunted mobility-for-all.

Score another point as a result of the fourth line being on-target.

That's four points for this quatrain.

In addition, the four lines all seem to pertain to the topic of driverless cars and offer a cohesive prediction about driverless cars and their advent.

Bonus point earned!

There it is, in all its glory.

Nostradamus had predicted the advent and prevalence of true self-driving cars, and the quatrain earns the vaunted score of five points.

Conclusion

Is he off his rocker?

I know that some might be outraged or even enraged that the quatrain in question has been matched to the emergence of driverless cars.

Let's just agree that it is an interesting thought to ponder.

Besides getting you to think about Nostradamus and the nature and aptness of his predictions, this discussion also serves to have us all seriously consider what the world will be like once we do have driverless cars.

Are we ready for that world?

What changes might occur and what should we do to prepare for them?

Nostradamus didn't seem to offer recommendations about how society should prepare for or deal with his predictions.

That seems to be up to us.

Setting aside whether the quatrain is relevant, as a society, are we ready for the day when driverless cars are all around us?

That seems to be up to us.

CHAPTER 7

ADVANCED DRIVING AND AI SELF-DRIVING CARS

CHAPTER 7

ADVANCED DRIVING AND
AI SELF-DRIVING CARS

Are you a good driver?

Your answer depends upon what the phrase "good driver" means.

Across the United States, each state provides various licensing requirements for those that want the privilege to drive a car.

Keep in mind that driving is considered a privilege and not some form of constitutional right. If you abuse the driving privilege, such as by committing a transgression against prevailing driving laws, your privilege to drive can be revoked.

The ability to get a driver's license is so easy that those in their mid-teens can qualify to drive in most states, though there might be restrictions about late-night driving and other facets.

In any case, when you ponder the aspect of obtaining a driver's license, as a society we have generally agreed to allow a minimum level of driving skills for anyone that wants to be able to legally drive a car on our public roadways.

Novice teenage drivers are often given a wide berth by other drivers that realize there is a newbie at the wheel. Those newcomer drivers are apt to brake suddenly or make a dangerous left turn, and otherwise are still figuring out how to control and properly drive a car.

Driving a car is a serious task.

You have at your command a multi-ton vehicle that can harm others and harm yourself. If you aren't paying attention, you can run over a pedestrian or ram into a cyclist. If you aren't comfortable with making tight turns you could swing wide while making a right turn and bash into a car next to you. And so on.

Over time, people get used to driving and usually become better at it, but there's no way of knowing how many people are especially good at driving versus those that continue to struggle at driving. If you perchance can avoid hitting people or smashing into a pole, you are considered by silent admission to be a good enough driver.

We are a nation of apparently *good enough* drivers (there are about 225 million licensed drivers in the United States).

Would we have the 40,000 car crash deaths per year and the estimated 1.2 million car-related crash injuries though if we were all possibly *better* drivers?

It's hard to say, but one would certainly assume so.

Car crash incidents are typically associated with drivers that are inattentive, or that are intoxicated, or that have some other matter undermining their driving prowess. We don't quite know whether those drivers would do a better job at driving and have avoided those incidents if they had stronger driving skills.

Of course, you could argue that if they did have stronger driving skills, they would possibly be more attentive and less likely to get behind the wheel in an untoward condition. Perhaps drivers that have a greater sense of how to drive might make driving even more seriously than they might otherwise.

Plus, there are certainly some number of car crashes that could have been averted if the driver did have a more robust driving skillset.

For those situations that involve having the car slide on a slippery road, or when taking a turn that the driver lost control of the vehicle, it could be that a driver with a more advanced skillset could have avoided the resulting calamity.

Indeed, imagine if all drivers had advanced level driving skills, akin to say a high-performance car driver.

All drivers would be proficient in driving skills that could be leveraged to avoid car crashes and thus aid in lowering the volume of lamentable car-related deaths and injuries that occur each year.

Not only would you be better able to avoid your own car mishaps, it would mean that there is an increased chance that you could avoid getting entangled with some other driver that has gone awry.

Presumably, all drivers would be safer drivers due to having an improved ability at driving a car, and it would also mean that when some driver does happen to falter, other nearby drivers might be able to get out of their way.

Unfortunately, we don't require everyday drivers in the United States to be versed in advanced driving skills.

If you can keep out of driving trouble, and upon periodic renewal of your driver's license you are able to retake successfully the minimum-level driving test, you can continue to drive in your ongoing muddling manner.

No need to comprehend the principles of tire adhesion and how your tires are crucial to staying on the road. No need to know how to best deal with a car that goes into a spin. There's no requirement to understand how weight transfer occurs during acceleration, and nor realize how your use of the gas pedal and the brake can simultaneously function in a coordinated manner to gain greater control of the car.

Sadly, our society has decided that you don't really need to know how to fully drive a car, at least not to the degree that a high-performance driver does.

You could argue that this unwillingness to up the ante on statutory driving requirements makes some sense from an overall economic perspective. The nationwide cost of having every driver take an advanced driving course and be forced to pass it to become a licensed driver would be a doozy of a price. You'd probably see people go up in arms over the added requirement.

One notable thought is whether the estimated national cost of $871 billion that annually goes toward car accidents could be reduced by requiring today's drivers to be more proficient in driving. And, let's not forget that the dollars cost doesn't include the lost lives and disrupted lives due to injuries from car crashes.

Okay, so we know, and can hopefully all agree that we have a preponderance of drivers that are minimally "good enough" to drive, and likely very few that have advanced driving skills akin to a high-performance driver. It seems apparent that any attempt to push those human drivers to a heightened skill level would be arduous and quite unlikely.

It seems like an unsolvable problem.

Wait a second, what about the advent of driverless cars?

Here's a worthwhile question: *Would we be wise to ensure that true self-driving cars have high-performance driving skills as an integral part of their AI driving capabilities?*

I say the answer is yes, very much so.

Let's unpack the matter and see.

The Levels Of Self-Driving Cars

It is important to clarify what I mean when referring to true self-driving cars.

True self-driving cars are ones that the AI drives the car entirely on its own and there isn't any human assistance during the driving task.

These driverless cars are considered a Level 4 and Level 5, while a car that requires a human driver to co-share the driving effort is usually considered at a Level 2 or Level 3. The cars that co-share the driving task are described as being semi-autonomous, and typically contain a variety of automated add-ons that are referred to as ADAS (Advanced Driver-Assistance Systems).

There is not yet a true self-driving car at Level 5, which we don't yet even know if this will be possible to achieve, and nor how long it will take to get there.

Meanwhile, the Level 4 efforts are gradually trying to get some traction by undergoing very narrow and selective public roadway trials, though there is controversy over whether this testing should be allowed per se (we are all life-or-death guinea pigs in an experiment taking place on our highways and byways, some point out).

Since semi-autonomous cars require a human driver, the adoption of those types of cars won't be markedly different than driving conventional cars, though there are some upsides and downsides worth considering.

Sure, Level 2 and Level 3 capabilities can aid a human driver and potentially enhance their driving skills, but the human can still overtake the driving controls and easily undermine the ADAS.

Furthermore, many of the ADAS features can be turned off by a driver, which some assert should not be allowed since presumably the ADAS is there to bolster the driver.

As I've repeatedly exhorted, we are headed into dangerous territory whereby human drivers won't fully comprehend what the car's automation is doing, and this lack of a theory of mind when you have a co-sharing driving arrangement, namely a human driver and a piece of automation that's not sufficiently sophisticated, portends that there will be severe gaps in understanding that are going to lead to car accidents.

For semi-autonomous cars, it is equally important that I mention a disturbing aspect that's been arising, namely that in spite of those human drivers that keep posting videos of themselves falling asleep at the wheel of a Level 2 or Level 3 car, we all need to avoid being misled into believing that the driver can take away their attention from the driving task while driving a semi-autonomous car.

You are the responsible party for the driving actions of the car, regardless of how much automation might be tossed into a Level 2 or Level 3.

Self-Driving Cars And High-Performance Driving

For Level 4 and Level 5 true self-driving cars, there won't be a human driver involved in the driving task.

All occupants will be passengers.

Today's efforts toward developing true self-driving cars are nearly entirely focused on the everyday driving task.

People want a driverless car that can take them over to their local grocery store. This involves successfully navigating neighborhood streets without hitting any children or meandering dogs and gently getting the passengers over to the mall.

Even freeway driving is considered a somewhat everyday driving task for the AI, namely that the AI needs to be able to get onto and off the freeway and stay properly within the lanes while on the freeway.

This is tantamount to what any average "good enough" human driver can do.

Should the aim be higher?

It's an easy argument to contend that certainly, we would want the AI to be more than simply a good enough driver.

If the AI could be infused with a high-performance driver skillset, imagine how much better off we would all be.

Presumably, the driverless car would be better at dealing with situations such as slick roadways or situations wherein another car veered suddenly toward the self-driving car.

Some automakers and self-driving tech firms are so overwhelmed with getting the everyday driving nailed down that trying to venture into advanced high-performance driving is considered an edge problem. Edge problems are a kind of industry parlance referring to driving scenarios that are categorized as at the edge of the solution space being solved, often also called corner cases.

Any reasonable AI developer for driverless cars would agree that it would be a nice-to-have of embodying high-performance driving skills, but they would also wince and say that we need to first crawl before we can walk.

In other words, the prevailing view is that once self-driving cars can be the equivalent of a human "good enough" driver, we can then turn our attention toward more advanced aspects such as high-performance driving skills.

The counterargument is that by not including high-performance driving skills now, we are gradually allowing onto our roadways a herd of cars that are unable to drive at a peak level.

Will the passengers inside a driverless car realize that their self-driving car is not a "topnotch" driver and only an "everyday" driver?

There are lawyers already lining up to make the case that if a self-driving car gets into a car accident, and if it had not been infused with high-performance driving skills which might have avoided the crash, the automaker or tech firm ought to be sued for not having appropriately skilled the AI.

A presumed defense would be that the AI contained a necessary and sufficient skillset to drive on public roadways, and in the desire to make progress on self-driving cars, it was a necessity to start there.

The counterclaim might further be extended that if there had been an attempt to include high-performance driving skills, it would have delayed the advent of driverless cars.

It would be straightforward too by the respondent to point to the other driverless car makers and note that their self-driving cars by-and-large also lack high-performance driving capabilities.

We'll have to wait and see if those defensive postures are adequate.

The general public might not buy into such arguments and be disappointed and outright disturbed to discover that the vaunted driverless cars they've been riding in were not at a level beyond everyday drivers.

Taking a slightly different angle on the topic, those automakers or tech firms that opt to implant high-performance driving skills into their driverless cars can leverage the facet by pointing it out as a strategic differentiator.

If you believe that all self-driving cars will essentially be alike, meaning that consumers and riders won't distinguish any one type of driverless car from another, it might be notable for a self-driving car maker to emphasize that their AI is a better driver or at least more skilled at driving.

Of course, this differentiation might also raise people's eyebrows as they suddenly become aware that apparently some driverless cars have advanced driving skills, and some don't.

Regulators might be prodded into action to establish requirements for the AI driving skillsets that are to be used in driverless cars.

Conclusion

Don't misinterpret these remarks to suggest that there aren't efforts underway of adding high-performance driving skills into self-driving cars.

There are indeed those kinds of efforts taking place.

In fact, the recently released NOVA documentary entitled "Look Who's Driving" (see my review here) briefly showcased such an effort taking place at Stanford University. Stanford Professor Chris Gerdes and the team at their Center for Automotive Research (CARS) lab have been exploring the inclusion of high-performance driving skills into self-driving cars.

And, let's be clear, most of the automakers and self-driving tech firms have on their To-Do lists these kinds of skill sets and are eager to pursue those elements.

It's a question of trying to crawl before you walk, or to some degree perhaps mixing the two together, the crawling and the walking. You see, the definition of high-performance driving skills is so loose that you could argue that some of the presumed everyday driving skills being imbued into driverless cars are in the same ballpark as high-performance driving.

There are some added twists involved in imbuing high-performance driving skills into the AI.

If you just toss the high-performance driving skills into an existing set of everyday driving skills, you could end up in a situation of dueling driving actions. When a slippery road is encountered, the everyday driving skillset might refuse to handover to the high-performance skillset, and the driverless car either fails to leverage the added feature or maybe hands-over control belatedly.

In that sense, the high-performance skillset needs to be seamlessly implanted within the overarching AI driving skillset.

Another difficulty involves the classic Trolley Problem that faces driverless car makers. The Trolley Problem refers to an ethical debate about how and when the AI ought to make driving decisions that involve life-or-death choices (see my detailed explanation here).

Here's how that applies.

Suppose the high-performance driving capability could whip around the driverless car and potentially avoid slamming into a wall, perhaps coping with a patch of black ice on the roadway. If there are passengers inside the driverless car, the act of making such a radical movement could injure them, causing a whiplash effect. On the other hand, slamming into the wall is going to injure them too.

Which is the right choice, make the radical move or allow the car to smash into the wall?

Many such scenarios can be crafted that are not perhaps so clear cut as to which choice is the better one.

One final twist for now.

Should the human passengers be allowed to invoke the high-performance driving skillset of the AI system?

You are in your nifty sports car that is driverless. Deciding to go up into the mountains, you wonder how it might do on the upcoming mountainous roads. You tell the Natural Language Processing (NLP) element of the AI driving system to go ahead and punch it.

Hey, you think to yourself, let's see what this baby can do, and invoke the high-performance driving capability to speedily take those curves and give you a thrill ride.

As a society, do we want passengers to be able to activate such a mode?

It's an open question.

Well, overall, I've tried to bring to your attention that self-driving cars are eventually going to have high-performance driving skills, which bodes well for us all, though the timing of getting those skills into the AI and making sure that they work appropriately will be a tough road to travel.

Say, is that driverless car over there peeling out and shredding it tires?

Could be.

CHAPTER 8

CYBERTRUCK

WINDOWS SHATTERED

MYSTERY

CHAPTER 8

CYBERTRUCK
WINDOWS SHATTERED
MYSTERY

Some refer to the incident as windowgate.

Jokes and memes aplenty have arisen, and the media headlines touted that expectations were shattered, along with records being smashed.

Of course, I'm referring to the big unveiling last week of Tesla's new Cybertruck, a pickup truck that's an EV (Electrical Vehicle) and made with all sorts of armored plating and bulletproof windows (well, maybe; more about that in a moment).

With rather prominent acute angles and an overall trapezoidal shape, this sci-fi looking vehicle generated both great praise and condemnation.

Comparisons of the truck's unusual look were immediately tweeted with examples from Star Wars to children's cartoons.

Some asserted that this design is exactly what the world needs, while others expressed qualms that it portends for more car accidents due to potentially poor visibility and the chances of driving it like an imposing military tank.

The Moment Of True Surprise

Besides the bright lights and splashy manner of doing the reveal, there was an OMG (Oh My Gosh) moment that got perhaps as much media coverage as did the fact that this is Musk's latest creation to be brought to our attention.

I'll walk you through what happened (though many of you have likely seen the video of the incident, which became the darling of online videos for about a day or two).

As part of the showcase about the armored aspects, a sledgehammer was used to whack at the driver's side door, seemingly bouncing off the outer skin of the Cybertruck and impacting with little or no visible damage.

It was one of those moments that anyone showcasing a new product is eager to do, vividly illustrating what has been said verbally during the unveiling and offering seemingly irrefutable proof of the pledge made about the product.

The next step was potentially a bridge too far.

Musk implored his key designer of the Cybertruck to throw a small steel ball at the driver's side window, presumably demonstrating the bulletproof nature of the glass.

Curiously, the designer seemed to somewhat question the directive, asking "Sure?" in a subtle way, and yet upon Musk's added urging the deed was undertaken.

I mention that this hesitation seems curious since the tossing act was most likely tried beforehand and therefore, they would have known that the outcome was going to be good, i.e., no broken glass. Why hesitate if you know for sure that it will go well and provide the visual evidence to support the touted claims?

Now, that being said, sometimes, as part of a demo, you might feign concern, raising up the ante and getting the audience on the edge of their seats. I don't think that's what was going on, and it seemed like a genuine form of hesitation, as though the designer might have suspected that somehow the toss could cause a problem.

Akin to the question of whether there was another shooter on the grassy knoll, you can readily study the videotapes of the Cybertruck demo, closely examining each frame, if you think it might help to figure out the unvarnished truth.

In any case, upon tossing the steel ball at the window, the ball dramatically smacked and cracked the glass, leaving the kind of fracture that you'd maybe see after a bullet hits and shatters a plate of glass.

Oops.

Not at all what one might expect from a repeatedly pumped-up declaration that the windows were fully and completely bulletproof. This is not the kind of result that builds confidence in the words spoken about a new product.

There was a sense of collective shock by the audience and Musk himself was heard to utter "Oh my f------- God," an expression seemingly exhibiting surprise and dismay.

Anyone that has ever had a demo go awry will know exactly what Musk must have been feeling at that moment. The range of emotions is from being crestfallen to abject disappointment, often followed by being irked and upset that this could have happened at the worst of times (during a grand reveal).

Many an executive has shifted into a heads-will-roll mode the instant they come off the stage when calamities occur during a highly visible demo.

On the stage, there was no place to hide and no means to pretend that the glass hadn't shattered. The audience attending saw it happen, as did a large global audience that was watching via live streaming.

What would you do?

Since there's no means to undo the shattering, you might as well double down and try tossing the ball at the passenger's window. Your hope upon hopes is that the second toss won't result in a smashed window.

You could then try to make the first window shattering seem to be a fluke. And, you could point to the second window as evidence that the glass is unbreakable. Plus, you might (desperately) try a Yoda-like mind trick of getting the audience to focus on the unbroken window and forget that they can also see the smashed one too.

Musk opted to have the design lead proceed to do the second toss.

Yikes, the glass broke on the passenger's window too.

Two strikes, and in this case, you are out.

When a demo has troubles, you usually try to talk your way around the matter. There's not much else you can do.

It would have made no sense to have the Cybertruck driven off the stage to get it out of view. The Cybertruck was sitting there, in all its glory, showing off the design and armor, along with having two shattered windows.

Musk tried to overcome the embarrassing snafu by pointing out that the steel ball at least had not gone into the interior of the vehicle and thus had not fully penetrated the window.

Also, he assured the audience that the Tesla team had tested the windows many times, including tossing everything at it in a proverbial "kitchen sink" exhaustive method of testing. Furthermore, just a few minutes earlier they had dropped steel balls onto window plates, right there on the stage, and it sure seemed to showcase the sturdiness of the glass (no breakage apparent).

Any prominent demo that has something go awry of that magnitude is likely to get attention, especially when there was so much other showmanship being employed.

Those that have had their lives filled with doing demos know that you often lay up late at night the evening before a new product launch. You pray that every conceivable aspect has been tied down. There is usually a huge preparation effort beforehand and the prior practice gives you faith that things will hopefully go well.

Yet, despite all such preparations, there is always the chance of a demo glitch.

If there is going to be a glitch, you have in the back of your mind that maybe it will happen on something inconsequential.

Or, when the hitch occurs, you think about ways to quickly move ahead in the demo and act as though nothing untoward occurred. Luck might be with you that the audience won't notice the glitch or that they might assume it was part of the demo effort and not a gotcha moment.

For the Tesla Cybertruck, the broken glass became as much of the top story about the unveiling as did the pickup truck itself.

The incident will go down in the history of car demos, adding to prior well-known glitches that have happened during new vehicle unveilings.

Stuff happens, as they say.

To date, there is not a definitive answer as to why the windows shattered.

It is an unsolved mystery.

Let's see if we can come up with potential reasons to explain the snafu.

The Top Ten Reasons

We could postulate a myriad of reasons that the glass shattered.

I've boiled them down into the Top 10.

Here they are:

1. Was Done On Purpose

Some have speculated that the shattered glass was a purposeful outcome, done as a public relations stunt. In short, Tesla and Musk intentionally planned to have the glass break.

It does seem to be the case that the smashed glass generated gobs more publicity than the unveiling alone might have otherwise garnered.

Nonetheless, I'm going to reject this reason based on the aspect that Musk and his designer seemed genuinely surprised (if it was an acting job, they both deserve an Oscar), and it seems doubtful that undermining your own words about the bulletproof elements would be worth the added newsworthiness.

2. Hindsight Revisionist Theory

You might recall the infamous case about how New Coke was brought out by the Coca-Cola company, doing so to great fanfare, and then got trounced that the New Coke was vastly inferior to the original Coke. After months of getting dinged, the original Coke was reinstated and the New Coke was essentially retired.

Some say that the Coke matter was a gigantic snafu, while others point out that Coke regained prominence and was able to leverage the incident to gain against competitors. As such, some suggest via a kind of historical hindsight revisionist viewpoint, it was all a clever ploy.

Well, even if via hindsight the shattered glass was a smart move, this still doesn't quite explain how it occurred.

Who planned it and who was in on the ruse?

Maybe Musk and the designer were kept out-of-the-loop and didn't know that the glass was going to break.

Or, maybe the designer knew about it (recall his "Sure?" comment), and he had cold feet at the moment of truth.

I'm going to reject these conspiracy type notions and suggest that it seems hard to imagine that the Tesla team would be willing to keep Musk in the dark about an intentional plan to have the glass break.

Musk is the kind of hands-on leader that would seem unlikely to take kindly to behind-his-back machinations of this enormity.

3. Glass Was Treated Backstage

One explanation for the glass breaking is that while the Cybertruck was backstage, awaiting being brought out, someone on the Tesla team decided to treat the glass or coat it with a special substance.

Perhaps the treatment was intended to make the glass look shiny.

You can certainly understand that someone could have opted to do so, hoping it would further enhance the ball throwing act that was planned for the on-stage performance. And, it might have been one of those last moment unplanned actions, for which the person doing it would have assumed that nothing bad could come from the coating.

Then, when the steel ball was tossed, somehow the coating or treatment made the glass more vulnerable and so it shattered.

If that's the case, what kind of coating or treatment could cause bulletproof glass to lose its strength to the degree that it would transmute from being virtually unbreakable to instead being readily smashed?

That's impressive chemistry.

Not ruling out this reason, but it seems like quite a stretch.

4. Prior Test Weakened The Glass

Sometimes, when you are getting ready to do a demo, you perform the demo, end-to-end, and do so just minutes before going on-stage.

The idea is that by performing the demo within moments of doing it again, on-stage, you are going to be reassured that everything is ready to go. This is worthy to consider. If a practice run-thru of the demo had taken place say a day before, you never know what changes might have happened in the interim, and therefore it makes sense to do one final demo at the last minute.

On the other hand, there are demos that often alter the product that is going to be demonstrated. For example, a classic bad move is when you run software that you are going to demo, and enter various fake values, which when you do the stage demo it now has those fake values already entered. Many software demos have been undermined by a last-minute run thru.

One possibility is that the Cybertruck was tested before the on-stage effort, perhaps having someone toss steel balls at the windows. The windows didn't shatter and so it was assumed they were working as anticipated. Meanwhile, hairline fractures occurred.

Thus, when the on-stage toss occurred, the glass was already in a weakened state.

Whoever decided to do the pre-test might not have realized that the pre-test itself could undermine the integrity of the glass. Though, you would think that during the initial testing process of the glass that they would have already discovered the aspect that such hairline fractures could arise and weaken the glass.

Maybe the person doing the last-minute test didn't know what other members of the test team knew.

This reason seems to have some legs to it.

5. Glass Weakened By Blow To The Car Door

A clever physics answer would be that the sledgehammer blow to the driver's door was enough to have led to a weakening of the glass window of the driver's door.

This seems plausible, though it does raise the question about the second window.

Why would the second window also be weakened?

Did a blow to the door somehow reverberate through the body of the car and cause two or more of the glass windows to become fractured?

Did the driver's side window becomes weakened by the blow, and somehow it then led to the second window becoming weaker?

Maybe, if one window that's adjacent to another window is smashed, it no longer can aid the adjacent window in not becoming smashed?

Again, it's one of those grassy knolls set of questions.

Let's keep this reason on the list but mark it as less likely.

6. Not The Right Glass

Perhaps someone put the wrong glass into the Cybertruck that was being used for the demo.

During the various testing of the Cybertruck prototypes, it is possible they were using bulletproof glass from vendor X and had other glass laying around from vendor Y. The vendor Y glass wasn't as strong as the glass of vendor X.

In an unfortunate mix-up, the Tesla team inadvertently put the glass Y into the Cybertruck that was destined to go on-stage.

From all appearances, suppose you couldn't readily discern any visual difference between the X and Y glass. It could be an easy mistake to have put the Y glass into the windows and not realized that you should have used X glass.

Though this is a tempting reason for the shattering of the windows, it would require that they had the wrong glass in-hand and put it into the windows of the demo Cybertruck, which is possible and yet somehow at the same time not fully plausible.

We'll keep it on the list.

7. The Toss Or Steel Ball Were Different

Tesla released a video of a toss by the head designer that occurred during the initial testing of the Cybertruck windows.

In the released video, the glass does not break.

Some have tried to analyze the tossing action.

It seems that per such analyses, the angle and thrusting force of the initial test are not the same as what occurred on-stage during the demo. As such, maybe the designer happened to inadvertently toss the steel balls in a different manner, doing so in a means on-stage that caused the glass to shatter.

We also don't know that the steel balls shown in the initial test video are the same as the steel balls used during the on-stage demo.

Furthermore, the initial test video shows various clamps and other contraptions on or nearby the glass window, perhaps steadying the glass or otherwise aiding the glass in being less likely to break.

The nature of toss and possibly in conjunction with different kinds of steel balls led to a grand convergence that made the glass smash during the live demo, some postulate.

Suspicious minds also have said that maybe Tesla is hiding other testing videos that show the glass breaking, and only released the one video of it not breaking (doing so to save face). This would be a fiendish way, they would argue, of convincing us that the glass really is unbreakable, when the truth is that Tesla possesses dozens of videos showing the glass breaking during testing (which, they probably do, since logically during testing often things break).

Setting aside the conspiracy theories, it seems hard to imagine that the tossing action would have been so different that it would suddenly break the glass.

Yes, I realize that the angle of the toss and how the ball struck the glass could make a difference, but somehow this does not seem a very satisfying answer.

8. Windows Improperly Placed

Suppose the glass windows of the on-stage Cybertruck were slightly askew.

Perchance someone inadvertently failed to roll the windows up entirely. A small and unnoticeable gap between the window and the door frame existed. Perhaps the bulletproof glass is only unbreakable as long as it is held in a steady state.

Another similar idea is that the glass windows were improperly fitted into the demo Cybertruck.

If they had not ever used the demo Cybertruck before, it could have been one that got some new windows put into it, and regrettably, the windows were not fitted appropriately.

Or, the Cybertruck had been used before, and when they put the "final" windows into it, the ones that would be used for the demo, darned if they messed-up fitting them into the frame.

9. Other-Worldly Explanation

This is a quick theory to recite.

Maybe there's some other-worldly explanation, as though some unseen hand opted to shatter the glass or weakened the glass so it would shatter.

Exorcism needed?

10. Murphy's Law

It seems almost undeniable that Murphy's Law of demos has once again reared its ugly head.

Whatever can go wrong during a demo, will go wrong.

Enough said.

Conclusion

There are your Top 10 reasons for the windowgate matter.

More reasons do exist, such as a juicy one that a competitor replaced the windows while the Tesla team wasn't looking. This kind of shenanigans occurs at college campuses during cross-town rivalry weeks, but it is hard to fathom that another automaker snuck into Tesla and managed to change the windows on the demo Cybertruck.

All in all, I guess I'll go with Murphy's Law, ever-present in all demos.

CHAPTER 9
ARTIFICIAL STUPIDITY
AND
AI SELF-DRIVING CARS

CHAPTER 9

ARTIFICIAL STUPIDITY
AND AI SELF-DRIVING CARS

When someone says that another person is intelligent, you pretty much assume that this is a praising of how smart or bright the other person might be.

In contrast, if someone is labeled as being stupid, there is a reflexive notion that the person is essentially unintelligent. Generally, the common definition of being stupid is that stupidity consists of a lack of intelligence.

This brings up a curious aspect.

Suppose we somehow had a bucket filled with intelligence. We are going to pretend that intelligence is akin to something tangible and that we can essentially pour it into and possibly out of a bucket that we happen to have handy.

Upon pouring this bucket filled with intelligence onto say the floor, what do you have left?

One answer is that the bucket is now entirely empty and there is nothing left inside the bucket at all. The bucket has become vacuous and contains absolutely nothing.

Another answer is that the bucket upon being emptied of intelligence has a leftover that consists of stupidity. In other words, once you've removed so-called intelligence, the thing that you have remaining is stupidity.

I realize this is a seemingly esoteric discussion but, in a moment, you'll see that the point being made has a rather significant ramification for many important things, including and particularly for the development and rise of Artificial Intelligence (AI).

Ponder these weighty questions:

- Can intelligence exist without stupidity, or in a practical sense is there always some amount of stupidity that must exist if there is also the existence of stupidity?

Some assert that intelligence and stupidity are zen-like yin and yang.

In this perspective, you cannot grasp the nature of intelligence unless you also have a semblance of stupidity as a kind of measuring stick.

It is said that humans become increasingly intelligent over time, and thus are reducing their levels of stupidity. You might suggest that intelligence and stupidity are playing a zero-sum game, namely that as your intelligence rises you are simultaneously reducing your level of stupidity (similarly, if perchance your stupidity rises, this implies that your intelligence lowers).

- Can humans arrive at a 100% intelligence and a zero amount of stupidity, or are we fated to always have some amount of stupidity, no matter how hard we might try to become fully intelligent?

Returning to the bucket metaphor, some would claim that there will never be the case that you are completely and exclusively intelligent and have expunged stupidity. There will always be some amount of stupidity that's sitting in that bucket.

If you are clever and try hard, you might be able to narrow down how much stupidity you have, though nonetheless there is still some amount of stupidity in that bucket, albeit perhaps at some kind of minimal state.

- Does having stupidity help intelligence or is it harmful to intelligence?

You might be tempted to assume that any amount of stupidity is a bad thing and therefore we must always be striving to keep it caged or otherwise avoid its appearance.

But we need to ask whether that simplistic view of tossing stupidity into the "bad" category and placing intelligence into the "good" category is potentially missing something more complex. You could argue that by being stupid, at times, in limited ways, doing so offers a means for intelligence to get even better.

When you were a child, suppose you stupidly tripped over your own feet, and after doing so, you came to the realization that you were not carefully lifting your feet. Henceforth, you became more mindful of how to walk and thus became intelligent at the act of walking. Maybe later in life, while walking on a thin curb, you managed to save yourself from falling off the edge of the curb, partially due to the earlier in life lesson that was sparked by stupidity and became part of your intelligence.

Of course, stupidity can also get us into trouble.

Despite having learned via stupidity to be careful as you walk, one day you decide to strut on the edge of the Grand Canyon. While doing so, oops, you fall off and plunge into the chasm.

Was it an intelligent act to perch yourself on the edge like that?

Apparently not.

As such, we might want to note that stupidity can be a friend or a foe, and it is up to the intelligence portion to figure out which is which in any given circumstance and any given moment.

You might envision that there is an eternal struggle going on between the intelligence side and the stupidity side.

On the other hand, you might equally envision that the intelligence side and stupidity side are pals, each of which tugs at the other, and therefore it is not especially a fight as it is a delicate dance and form of tension about which should prevail (at times) and how they can each moderate or even aid the other.

This preamble provides a foundation to discuss something increasingly becoming worthy of attention, namely the role of Artificial Intelligence and (surprisingly) the role of Artificial Stupidity.

Thinking Seriously About Artificial Stupidity

We hear every day about how our lives are being changed via the advent of Artificial Intelligence.

AI is being infused into our smartphones, and into our refrigerators, and into our cars, and so on.

If we are intending to place AI into the things we use, it begs the question as to whether we need to consider the yang of the yin, specifically do we need to be cognizant of Artificial Stupidity?

Most people snicker upon hearing or seeing the phrase "Artificial Stupidly," and they assume it must be some kind of insider joke to refer to such a thing.

Admittedly, the conjoining of the words artificial and stupidity seems, well, perhaps stupid in of itself.

But, by going back to the earlier discussion about the role of intelligence and the role of stupidity as it exists in humans, you can recast your viewpoint and likely see that whenever you carry on a discussion about intelligence, one way or another you inevitably need to also be considering the role of stupidity.

Some suggest that we ought to use another way of expressing Artificial Stupidity to lessen the amount of snickering that happens. Floated phrases include Artificial Unintelligence, Artificial Humanity, Artificial Dumbness, and others, none of which have caught hold as yet.

Please bear with me and accept the phrasing of Artificial Stupidity and also go along with the belief that it isn't stupid to be discussing Artificial Stupidity.

Indeed, you could make the case that the act of not discussing Artificial Stupidity is the stupid approach, since you are unwilling or unaccepting of the realization that stupidity exists in the real world and therefore in the artificial world of computer systems that are we attempting to recreate intelligence, you would be ignoring or blind to what is essentially the other half of the overall equation.

In short, some say that true Artificial Intelligence requires a combining of the "smart" or good AI that we think of today and the inclusion of Artificial Stupidity (warts and all), though the inclusion must be done in a smart way.

Indeed, let's deal with the immediate knee jerk reaction that many have of this notion by dispelling the argument that by including Artificial Stupidity into Artificial Intelligence you are inherently and irrevocably introducing stupidity and presumably, therefore, aiming to make AI stupid.

Sure, if you stupidly add stupidity, you have a solid chance of undermining the AI and rendering it stupid.

On the other hand, in recognition of how humans operate, the inclusion of stupidity, when done thoughtfully, could ultimately aid the AI (think about the story of tripping over your own feet as a child).

Here's something that might really get your goat.

Perhaps the only means to achieve true and full AI, which is not anywhere near to human intelligence levels to-date, consists of infusing Artificial Stupidity into AI; thus, as long as we keep Artificial Stupidity at arm's length or as a pariah, we trap ourselves into never reaching the nirvana of utter and complete AI that is able to seemingly be as intelligent as humans are.

Ouch, by excluding Artificial Stupidity from our thinking, we might be damming ourselves to not arriving at the pinnacle of AI.

That's a punch to the gut and so counter-intuitive that it often stops people in their tracks.

There are emerging signs that the significance of revealing and harnessing artificial stupidity (or whatever it ought to be called), can be quite useful.

At a recent talk sponsored by the Simons Institute for the Theory of Computing at the University of California Berkeley, I chatted with MIT Professor Andrew Lo and discussed his espoused clever inclusion of artificial stupidity into improving financial models, which he has done in recognition that human foibles need to be appropriately recognized and contended within the burgeoning field of FinTech.

His fascinating co-authored book *A Non-Random Walk Down Wall Street* is an elegant look at how human behavior is composed of both rationality and irrationality, giving rise to his theory, coined as the Adaptive Markets Hypothesis. His insightful approach goes beyond the prevailing bounds of how financial trading marketplaces do and can best operate.

Are there other areas or applications in which the significance of artificial stupidity might come to play?

Yes.

One such area, I assert, involves the inclusion of artificial stupidity into the advent of true self-driving cars.

Shocking?

Maybe so.

Let's unpack the matter.

Exploiting Artificial Stupidity For Gain

When referring to true self-driving cars, I'm focusing on Level 4 and Level 5 of the standard scale used to gauge autonomous cars. These are self-driving cars that have an AI system doing the driving and there is no need and typically no provision for a human driver.

The AI does all the driving and any and all occupants are considered passengers.

On the topic of Artificial Stupidity, it is worthwhile to quickly review the history of how the terminology came about.

In the 1950s, the famous mathematician and pioneering computer scientist Alan Turing proposed what has become known as the Turing test for AI.

Simply stated, if you were presented with a situation whereby you could interact with a computer system imbued with AI, and at the same time separately interact with a human too, and you weren't told beforehand which was which (let's assume they are both hidden from view), upon your making inquiries of each, you are tasked with deciding which one is the AI and which one is the human.

We could then declare the AI a winner as exhibiting intelligence if you could not distinguish between the two contestants. In that sense, the AI is indistinguishable from the human contestant and must ergo be considered equal in intelligent interaction.

There are some holes in this logic, which I provide a detailed analysis of here, in any case, the Turing test is widely used as a barometer for measuring whether or when AI might be truly achieved.

There is a twist to the original Turing test that many don't know about.

One qualm expressed was that you might be smarmy and ask the two contestants to calculate say pi to the thousandth digit.

Presumably, the AI would do so wonderfully and readily tell you the answer in the blink of an eye, doing so precisely and abundantly correctly. Meanwhile, the human would struggle to do so, taking quite a while to answer if using paper and pencil to make the laborious calculation, and ultimately would be likely to introduce errors into the answer.

Turing realized this aspect and acknowledged that the AI could be essentially unmasked by asking such arithmetic questions.

He then took the added step, one that some believe opened a Pandoras box, and suggested that the AI ought to avoid giving the right answers to arithmetic problems.

In short, the AI could try to fool the inquirer by appearing to answer as a human might, including incorporating errors into the answers given and perhaps taking the same length of time that doing the calculations by hand would take.

Starting in the early 1990s, a competition was launched that is akin to the Turing test, offering a modest cash prize and has become known as the Loebner Prize, and in this competition, the AI systems are typically infused with human-like errors to aid in fooling the inquirers into believing the AI is the human.

There is controversy underlying this, but I won't go into that herein. A now-classic article appeared in 1991 in *The Economist* about the competition.

Notice that once again we have a bit of irony that the introduction of stupidity is being done to essentially portray that something is intelligent.

This brief history lesson provides a handy launching pad for the next elements of this discussion.

Let's boil down the topic of Artificial Stupidity into two main facets or definitions:

1) Artificial Stupidity is the purposeful incorporation of human-like stupidity into an AI system, doing so to make the AI seem more human-like, and being done not to improve the AI per se but instead to shape the perception of humans about the AI as being seemingly intelligent.

2) Artificial Stupidity is an acknowledgment of the myriad of human foibles and the potential inclusion of such "stupidity" into or alongside the AI in a conjoined manner that can potentially improve the AI when properly managed.

One common misnomer that I'd like to dispel about the first part of the definition involves a somewhat false assumption that the computer potentially is going to purposefully miscalculate something.

There are some that shriek in horror and disdain that there might be a suggestion that the computer would intentionally seek to incorrectly do a calculation, such as figuring out pi but doing so in a manner that is inaccurate.

That's not what the definition necessarily implies.

It could be that the computer might correctly calculate pi to the thousandth digit, and then opt to tweak some of the digits, which it would say keep track of, and do this in a blink of the eye, and then wait to display the result after an equivalent of human-by-hand amount of time.

In that manner, the computer has the correct answer internally and has only displayed something that seems to have errors.

Now, that certainly could be bad for the humans that are relying upon what the computer has reported but note that this is decidedly not the same as though the computer has in fact miscalculated the number.

There's more than can be said about such nuances, but for now let's continue forward.

Both of those variants of Artificial Stupidity can be applied to true self-driving cars.

Doing so carries a certain amount of angst and will be worthwhile to consider.

Artificial Stupidity And True Self-Driving Cars

Today's self-driving cars that are being tried out on our public roadways have already gotten a reputation for their driving prowess. Overall, driverless cars to-date are akin to a novice teenage driver that is timid and somewhat hesitant about the driving task.

When you encounter a self-driving car, it will often try to create a large buffer zone between it and the car ahead, attempting to abide by the car lengths rule-of-thumb that you were taught when first learning to drive.

Human drivers generally don't care about the car lengths safety zone and edge up on other cars, doing so to their own endangerment.

Here's another example of driving practices.

Upon reaching a stop sign, a driverless car will usually come to a full and complete stop. It will wait to see that the coast is clear, and then cautiously proceed. I don't know about you, but I can say that where I drive, nobody makes complete stops anymore at stop signs. A rolling stop is the norm nowadays.

You could assert that humans are driving in a reckless and somewhat stupid manner. By not having enough car lengths between your car and the car ahead, you are increasing your chances of a rear-end crash. By not fully stopping at a stop sign, you are increasing your risks of colliding with another car or a pedestrian.

In a Turing test manner, you could stand on the sidewalk and watch cars going past you, and by their driving behavior alone you could likely ascertain which are the self-driving cars and which are the human-driven cars.

Does that sound familiar?

It should, since this is roughly the same as the arithmetic precision issue earlier raised.

How to solve this?

One approach would be to introduce Artificial Stupidity as defined above.

First, you could have the on-board AI purposely shorten the car's length buffer to appear as though it is driving in the same manner as humans. Likewise, the AI could be modified to roll through stop signs. This is all rather easily arranged.

Humans watching a driverless car and a human-driven car would no longer be able to discern one such car from the other since they both would be driving in the same error-laden way.

That seems to solve one problem as it relates to the perception that we humans might have about whether the AI of self-driving cars is intelligent or not.

But, wait a second, aren't we then making the AI into a riskier driver?

Do we want to replicate and promulgate this car-crash causing risky human driving behaviors?

Sensibly, no.

Thus, we ought to move to the second definitional portion of Artificial Stupidity, namely by incorporating these "stupid" ways of driving into the AI system in a substantive way that allows the AI to leverage those aspects when applicable and yet also be aware enough to avoid them or mitigate them when needed.

Rather than having the AI drive in human error-laden ways and do so blindly, the AI should be developed so that it is well-equipped enough to cope with human driving foibles, detecting those foibles and being a proper defensive driver, along with leveraging those foibles when the circumstances make sense to do so (for more on this, see my posting here).

Conclusion

One of the most unspoken secrets about today's AI is that it does not have any semblance of common-sense reasoning and in no manner whatsoever has the capabilities of overall human reasoning (many refer to such AI as Artificial General Intelligence or AGI).

As such, some would suggest that today's AI is closer to the Artificial Stupidity side of things than it is to the true Artificial Intelligence side of things.

If there is a duality of intelligence and stupidity in humans, presumably you will need a similar duality in an AI system if it is to be able to exhibit human intelligence (though, some say that AI might not have to be so duplicative).

On our roads today, we are unleashing so-called AI self-driving cars, yet the AI is not sentient and not anywhere close to being sentient.

Will self-driving cars only be successful if they can climb further up the intelligence ladder?

No one yet knows, and it's certainly not a stupid question to be asked.

CHAPTER 10

REVENUE ESTIMATES

OF

AI SELF-DRIVING CARS

CHAPTER 10
REVENUE ESTIMATES
OF
AI SELF-DRIVING CARS

How high is up?

That's the rhetorical question often posed when someone asks how much money self-driving cars will potentially be able to make.

Part of the willingness and enthusiasm of VC firms and major automakers to invest in driverless car tech is due to the belief that there is a huge pot of gold at the end of the self-driving car rainbow.

Estimates provided by automotive industry analysts are at times wildly all over the map in terms of the revenue potential. Some have pegged the number into the $500B range for annual revenues, while others say it is more akin to the $1T-$5T in big bucks making per year.

The initial scramble for putting down bets on driverless hardware and software startups has cooled somewhat, partially a result of the realization that the hyped timetable for achieving true self-driving cars is going to be longer than what many talking heads had gushed about.

Those eager and breathless investors that wanted to grab up land right away were oftentimes doing so with one eye closed, or maybe both eyes were shut and blissfully happy to blindly plunk down cash into anyone or anything that promised to soon-to-deliver driverless cars.

Driverless Kits Afoul

One of the most egregious such offerings involved those that said they could make a low-cost kit for transforming a conventional car into a self-driving car.

Imagine that!

In the United States alone, there are an estimated 250 million conventional cars.

If you could merely buy a kit at your local auto store, or maybe even at Best Buy, wouldn't it be tremendous to take home the kit, slap it onto your beat-up old jalopy, and voila, you'd now have yourself a genuine driverless car.

The shelves would be stripped clean of those kits and people across this country would be overnight letting the AI drive for them since they would have miraculously turned their cars into AI self-driving passenger-toting vehicles.

It's a wonderful world.

Of course, the reality is quite afield of that kit notion.

As I've repeatedly exhorted, you are not going to be able to shove a bunch of spiffy tech onto a conventional car and have it become a true self-driving car.

Most of the kits that have been floated into the marketplace involve allowing you to trick and jury-rig your car into using automation to steer the wheels and push the pedals, but this is a highly dangerous gambit and fortunately, not many people have fallen for the ruse.

In one sense, crafting a true self-driving car involves brain surgery, and letting the everyday consumer operate in such a capacity is raft with concerns and calamity.

By the way, conspiracy theorists argue that anyone that disses on the kit's possibilities is doing so to protect the man, the large corporations, and wants to prevent the little guy from being able to afford and have driverless cars. This was frequently used in the pitches for such kits.

All I can say is that I'd welcome finding a means to make driverless cars as inexpensive as possible and have a mobility-for-all advent, though this has to be done safely and with the realization that cars are multi-ton vehicles that can readily harm and kill, so whatever tech is used had better be darned good.

I realize the conspiracy believing camp will retort that I am obviously saying this as part of the conspiracy card-holding schemers.

Oh well, let's move on.

Back-Of-The-Envelope Approach

When you are sometimes faced with a situation involving an estimation problem, you can resort to using a back-of-the-envelope approach.

A now-classic question asked during job interviews for techies includes pressing them to craft an estimate of the number of manhole covers that there are in New York City (NYC).

The initial reaction to such a question is that it seems utterly irrelevant and an impossibility if one doesn't have to access to Google search or an equivalent to look-up the answer.

What you are supposed to do is (cleverly) make use of the fact that NYC is laid out on a grid pattern and by using the number of rows and columns, i.e., streets and avenues, you can readily use simple multiplication and arrive at a figure that approximates the manhole cover count (assuming that there is an average of one manhole cover per such intersecting point).

One caveat is that this question presumes the interviewee already knows that NYC is based on a grid shape and happens to know how many rows and columns there are, which is therefore biased toward those that perchance live or are especially familiar with New York.

Some interviewers are okay with a candidate not knowing those facets, as long as the candidate asks probing questions of the interviewer to ultimately ascertain the answer (but, how many of us are willing to ask questions of the interviewer in such a tense setting?).

Some say it's a rather awkward or untoward question to ask and merely makes an already uncomfortable interview an even more dismal experience.

Returning to the topic of back-of-the-envelope estimations, the notion is that you try to use overall indicators to arrive at a reasonably sound estimate.

The estimate might be off by a bit, perhaps a lot, yet at least you have some general number around which you can then carry on your noodling and use for various added considerations.

People that live their lives in a precise way are usually uncomfortable with back-of-the-envelope methods. For them, the idea of making sweeping assumptions and forgoing getting into the meaty details is antithetical to their world view.

Yes, back-of-the-envelope estimates can be rather raw and crude.

Yes, you ought to interpret such estimates with a grain of salt, or maybe a boxcar full of grain.

Yes, these kinds of estimates can be misused, and inadvertently take on a life of their own as a form of gospel.

Nonetheless, using a back-of-the-envelope technique can be instructive, along with getting the creative juices going and lead to or inspire others to dig deeper and come up with something that either has the underlying details to support the guess or that showcases that the guess was woefully inadequate.

With that important preamble, let's see if we can estimate via back-of-the-envelope the revenue potential for true self-driving cars.

Remember, please, it's just back-of-the-envelope.

The Levels Of Self-Driving Cars

It is important to clarify what I mean when referring to true self-driving cars.

True self-driving cars are ones that the AI drives the car entirely on its own and there isn't any human assistance during the driving task.

These driverless cars are considered a Level 4 and Level 5, while a car that requires a human driver to co-share the driving effort is usually considered at a Level 2 or Level 3. The cars that co-share the driving task are described as being semi-autonomous, and typically contain a variety of automated add-ons that are referred to as ADAS (Advanced Driver-Assistance Systems).

There is not yet a true self-driving car at Level 5, which we don't yet even know if this will be possible to achieve, and nor how long it will take to get there.

Meanwhile, the Level 4 efforts are gradually trying to get some traction by undergoing very narrow and selective public roadway trials, though there is controversy over whether this testing should be allowed per se (we are all life-or-death guinea pigs in an experiment taking place on our highways and byways, some point out).

Since semi-autonomous cars require a human driver, the adoption of those types of cars won't be markedly different than driving conventional cars, so I'm not going to include them in the back-of-the-envelope estimation for true self-driving cars.

For semi-autonomous cars, it is equally important that I mention a disturbing aspect that's been arising, namely that in spite of those human drivers that keep posting videos of themselves falling asleep at the wheel of a Level 2 or Level 3 car, we all need to avoid being misled into believing that the driver can take away their attention from the driving task while driving a semi-autonomous car.

You are the responsible party for the driving actions of the car, regardless of how much automation might be tossed into a Level 2 or Level 3.

Self-Driving Cars And Potential Revenue

For Level 4 and Level 5 true self-driving cars, there won't be a human driver involved in the driving task.

All occupants will be passengers.

Many have predicted that we'll have a mobility transformation and essentially become a mobility-as-a-service economy, shaped around ridesharing on steroids.

Some believe that only large companies such as the automakers and maybe the prominent ridesharing firms will own and operate driverless cars. This will be done based on large fleets of self-driving cars that they opt to establish and deploy.

Furthermore, other large companies that today have nothing to do with cars at all are predicted to jump into the self-driving car bonanza.

It would seem easy enough to accomplish. Buy a bunch of pricey driverless cars, put them onto an online sharing network, and count the money as those AI-driven cars do your bidding and give people rides.

I'm known as a somewhat contrarian since I claim that we'll still have individual ownership of such cars.

My logic is that there is potentially a lot of money to be made by owning and leveraging your own self-driving car, thus we all will have a monetary incentive to want to do so.

Why let only the big companies get the dough when the mom-and-pop can do so too (see my detailed explanation here)?

In any case, there doesn't seem to be any disagreement per se that mobility via driverless cars will become more friction-free and the advent of self-driving cars will be a mighty disruption to our society (hopefully, a positive disruption).

The roughly 70 billion annual hours that Americans spend driving their cars today will shift those drivers into becoming passengers. That's a lot of time opened-up for other activities, doing so while commuting in a self-driving car that's outfitted with Internet access and other goodies.

It seems fair to assume that riding in a driverless car won't be for free and you'll need to pay some price to do so.

What will be the price and how will it be calculated?

Nobody knows for sure.

How much will people ride in driverless cars?

Nobody knows for sure.

Well, maybe we can take a poke at this and come up with something.

Currently, in the United States alone, we rack-up an estimated 3.22T miles of driving annually. You might not have seen that statistic before, and upon reflection, it really is somewhat staggering. That's a lot of miles.

For a back-of-the-envelope estimation, let's go ahead and pretend that all those miles of travel would be shifted entirely to driverless cars.

Thus, we are going to make a series of assumptions that include the aspects of having only driverless cars and no conventional cars on our roadways, and that people will be going the same kind of distances that they did while they were drivers of cars, etc.

We'll come back to those assumptions momentarily.

What kind of price might we come up with as a per-mile fee for using a driverless car?

Today's estimates tend to suggest that ridesharing via the use of human drivers is around $1.00 or more on a per-mile price (this can be higher and lower in some locales and various times of the year), and some pundits have predicted that the per-mile price for driverless cars is going to be about one-third of that amount, so let's use $0.35 as a round number.

By the simplest of math, we can calculate this:

- $1.12T annual revenue = 3.2T annual miles x $0.35 per mile fee

In the broadest of manners, we now have an estimate of the annual revenue that could be derived by self-driving cars.

It's a tad over a trillion dollars.

If you compare that estimated number to published charts of the annual revenue of various industries in the United States, the revenue of self-driving cars would be near the top of the chart and be on par with the real estate industry and other gigantic industries.

That's nice.

It also showcases why there are big companies eyeing the driverless car evolution. There does seem to be a pot of gold at the rainbow, really, for real, and not just a mirage.

The question today is how long will it take to reach the pot of gold and whether you can stomach making the investment now that will gradually and eventually turn to gold, but meanwhile, it is pretty much all R&D and not something that's turning a buck right away.

With our business culture being seemingly run by quarterly reports, it is hard to stay the course on an investment that seems attractive and yet it is bleeding money for now, and perhaps for quite a while ahead.

You've got to have some pretty strong and visionary guts to keep in the game.

This is not for the faint of heart.

There's More To The Estimation

I've mentioned that the 70 billion hours of driving time today will become 70 billion hours of sitting inside a driverless car.

This is worthy of consideration as it offers some additional and quite promising revenue opportunities.

Think of the advertising possibilities!

You'll have people trapped inside their self-driving cars, which I mean in a positive way, suggesting that they will be riding around in self-driving cars and presumably have nothing to do since they no longer need to be attentive to the driving task.

Plus, driverless cars will be outfitted internally with various LED displays so that you can watch video streaming via the 5G (and greater) online access to the Internet.

Advertisers will salivate at this prospective market potential.

Beam your ads into those driverless cars, capturing the attention of the riders, and you can use both short-form ads and longer-form ads (if the average commute time says 30 minutes to an hour, just imagine how much ad time that allows for).

There are lots of ways to further monetize driverless cars, including in-car online entertainment and infotainment, IoT access, and so on.

For the moment, it seems reasonable to push upward the $1.12T by suggesting that there will be at least new ad dollars arising via self-driving cars too. We don't know how much money that will bring in, but let's just use 20% on top of the existing estimate, and we'll go with an expanded revenue of say $1.34T.

Another facet to consider is the likelihood of induced demand to appear.

Induced demand refers to the notion that once you make something available, there might be additional demand that comes out of the woodwork that otherwise was suppressed.

Some believe that driverless cars will make finally a mobility-for-all world possible.

Perhaps the number of miles driven today is too low a base to use since it doesn't account for the induced demand that will be unleashed via driverless cars.

Also, the number of miles driven in the United States has been rising lately on the amount of about 2.8% per year, therefore by the time that driverless cars are prevalent we might be consuming a lot more miles than we are today.

As a side note, let's not deal with future dollars and for ease of discussion calculate everything in today's dollars, which notably ignores inflation and other economic elements that will impact future dollars.

Let's uplift the number of miles from 3.22T by perhaps 20% for an overall increase in ridership over the next several years and then another 20% for the anticipated induced demand, so overall boosting the 3.22T by about 40%, turning it into 4.50T, and then use our $0.35, producing $1.58T, and then toss-in the ads too, landing us at a revenue of around $1.89T.

We could also play with the $0.35 and raise it up since there is the possibility of charging more for driverless cars.

Please don't bicker and grumble about those numbers, since it's once again our back-of-the-envelope approach.

All-told, we seem to be arriving at a number of at least between $1T to $2T.

Is this reasonable?

You might have seen some pundits that have estimated in the $5T to $7T range, which is generally aligned with my estimates herein since those larger predictions are based on a global or worldwide estimate.

Yes, keep in mind that so far I've only discussed the United States market potential, yet one would be wise to see the larger picture of the massive size of the international markets too.

Conclusion

One of the frequent jokes made about the act of making assumptions is that when you "assume" it makes a "mule" out of you and me (there's a different word that goes in place of the word mule, I'm trying to keep things clean).

A rather imposing assumption is that we would have all driverless cars and no conventional cars on our roadways. I've said over and over that the rollout of driverless cars is going to take place over many years, likely decades.

Thus, arriving at the back-of-the-envelope $1T or more of revenue is quite some distance in the future.

As part of this noodling exercise, I decided to come beyond my scrawled envelope and put together a handy spreadsheet that includes a gradual build-up of driverless cars, starting at 0.01% of today's volume of cars and then reaching milestones such as 1% of all cars, 5% of all cars, 10%, 20%, 50%, 75%, 80%, 95%, 99%, and it suggests that once we reach a 50% mixture we'll cross the $500B mark and only reach the vaunted trillion dollars once we get above 75%.

I also included time, trying to anticipate when this will all emerge.

Once again, it's all back-of-the-envelope based, and the inclusion of a spreadsheet doesn't of itself make the numbers more magical.

Also, there's the allied question of how many driverless cars we will need on our roadways to sustain the incurring of those 3.22T or more miles, which is a topic that I'll be covering in a later column.

Generally, most believe that we won't need 250 million cars and instead can provide sufficient coverage by a lower number of cars, which I also agree with.

Another aspect is what will be the costs associated with deploying a driverless car (I've supported the notion that most driverless cars will only last about 4 years in-service due to the heightened usage demands).

Anyway, I've laid down the gauntlet now on the revenue matter.

You can already hear the pens and pencils and keyboards clacking by the swarms of industry analysts that are comparing their numbers to the numbers used here, and I'm sure that many have very sophisticated multi-dimensional statistical models to support their estimations.

That's great!

In this case, I hope you don't mind that I used the simpler back-of-an-envelope, yes, in this case, an actual envelope, which I happened to have laying around from my daily snail-mail bag.

Turns out that the back of the envelope was more interesting than the contents of the envelope.

Lance B. Eliot

158

CHAPTER 11

SURVIVALISTS

AND

AI SELF-DRIVING CARS

CHAPTER 11

SURVIVALISTS

AND

AI SELF-DRIVING CARS

Survivalists.

The word by itself conjures up quite a number of vivid images and a middling of controversy.

Some refer to survivalists as preppers, a term suggesting that there is intense preparation that goes into being ready to survive (please note that there's an ongoing dispute over whether the two monikers are the same or mean different things).

Generally, the viewpoint most have of these survivalists or preppers is that they are imbued with a belief that society is going to somehow breakdown and we'll have chaos in our streets.

Furthermore, under the unshakable faith of that belief, these ardent believers are getting ready for that day to arrive.

For them, it is just a matter of when and not a matter of "if" the reprehensible day shall arrive.

The everyday public tends to shake their head in modest disdain for those that live on the precipice of expecting the world to collapse. Silly, misguided, confused, and outright nutty is the typical refrain about the more vocal and visible survivalists around us.

A counterargument oftentimes employed is that people prepare for all kinds of disasters, including for example here in California we overtly prepare for earthquakes.

For example:

- You can buy earthquake insurance via the non-profit publicly established California Earthquake Authority to cover your housing and allied property for damages due to earthquakes.

- You can shore-up your shelves and picture frames by attaching them securely to the wall of your abode.

- You can figure out beforehand the safest place to be in your home during a shaker, being ready for a bone-rattling earthquake, and set up an escape plan with your family as to how you'll get out of the house if it starts to turn into rubble.

In short, millions of Californians that are preparing for such a disaster are "survivalists" in the sense that they are anticipating something untoward will happen and they are getting ready for that dire moment.

That being said, it turns out that only about 10% of Californians buy earthquake insurance and the remaining 90% seem to not be overly concerned about getting such insurance.

How many Californians are truly ready for an earthquake, other than perhaps knowing the infamous "drop, cover, and hold-on" mantra that is repeatedly taught in our elementary schools?

Likely not many.

For true survivalists, they would tend to point out that this lack of adequate preparation for an earthquake is exactly why they are getting ready, wanting to be one of those that will survive a calamity while the rest of society gets caught ill-prepared and presumably will perish or certainly falter when the worst-of-times arises.

Getting Ready For The Worst Of Times

One of the key elements involved in being a survivalist is setting up a survival retreat, perhaps an underground bunker someplace or a hidden shack that's off the beaten path and far from the societal turmoil that's coming.

They even have a so-called Bug-Out Bag (B.O.B.), also known as a Get Out Of Dodge (G.O.O.D.) kit, containing the essential items that they want to take with them to their survival retreat.

When the Stuff Hits The Fan (S.H.T.F.), note that I've cleaned-up that phrase a tad, the survivalist or prepper will have handy their essential items and be zipping along right away as they scurry to reach their prepared survival retreat.

This brings up another make-or-break element of being ready.

How will the person get from wherever they are to the place of their survival hut?

The odds are that where they currently undertake their normal day-to-day existence is quite a distance from the designated survival locale. Thus, walking to their retreat or riding a bicycle to get there is probably not a viable option.

Pretty much, most survivalists are planning to drive to their safety hideaway.

Indeed, a well-prepared prepper has a Bug-Out Vehicle (BOV).

Their BOV is usually a car that's been made into something more amenable to the grand getaway that's going to be needed.

What do you need for your escape vehicle?

A few key aspects include having sturdy tires since you'll most likely need to drive over roadway debris and maybe go off-road during your journey. You'll want extra gasoline since the prospects of gas stations being open and having available gas is going to be chancy.

The car needs to be in good shape. It won't do you any good if your escape vehicle is worn out and might breakdown the instant you get on your way.

Using a rooftop rack or carrier is going to be handy since you'll want to pile your crucial belongings and spare emergency supplies onto the top of the car if you have time to do so and can manage the act without jeopardizing the escape timing.

This brings up an interesting question: *Will the advent of true self-driving cars be helpful as a means of having an at-the-ready a Bug-Out Vehicle or will driverless cars be an ill-advised way to escape?*

The answer is that self-driving cars are going to be a dreadful choice of chariot when seeking to ride to safety, and thus survivalists are going to need to be prepared for some other means of transport.

If you are unclear why driverless cars are going to be such a confounding sticking point, I'd like to offer some thoughts on why that will be the case.

Let's unpack the matter.

The Levels Of Self-Driving Cars

It is important to clarify what I mean when referring to true self-driving cars.

True self-driving cars are ones that the AI drives the car entirely on its own and there isn't any human assistance during the driving task.

These driverless cars are considered a Level 4 and Level 5, while a car that requires a human driver to co-share the driving effort is usually considered at a Level 2 or Level 3. The cars that co-share the driving task are described as being semi-autonomous, and typically contain a variety of automated add-ons that are referred to as ADAS (Advanced Driver-Assistance Systems).

There is not yet a true self-driving car at Level 5, which we don't yet even know if this will be possible to achieve, and nor how long it will take to get there.

Meanwhile, the Level 4 efforts are gradually trying to get some traction by undergoing very narrow and selective public roadway trials, though there is controversy over whether this testing should be allowed per se (we are all life-or-death guinea pigs in an experiment taking place on our highways and byways, some point out).

Since semi-autonomous cars require a human driver, the adoption of those types of cars won't be markedly different than driving conventional cars, so I'm not going to include them in the discussion about having them used as a survivalist escape vehicle.

For semi-autonomous cars, it is equally important that I mention a disturbing aspect that's been arising, namely that in spite of those human drivers that keep posting videos of themselves falling asleep at the wheel of a Level 2 or Level 3 car, we all need to avoid being misled into believing that the driver can take away their attention from the driving task while driving a semi-autonomous car.

You are the responsible party for the driving actions of the car, regardless of how much automation might be tossed into a Level 2 or Level 3.

Self-Driving Cars And Escaping Chaos

For Level 4 and Level 5 true self-driving cars, there won't be a human driver involved in the driving task.

All occupants will be passengers.

Many have predicted that we'll have a mobility transformation and essentially become a mobility-as-a-service economy, shaped around ridesharing on steroids.

Some believe that only large companies such as the automakers and maybe the prominent ridesharing firms will own and operate driverless cars. This will be done based on large fleets of self-driving cars that they opt to establish and deploy.

So far, this seems just dandy and doesn't appear to run afoul of the desire to use a driverless car as your survivalist escape transport.

In theory, you could use your smartphone to request a ridesharing self-driving car, tell the AI to hit the gas and get going, and then sit back in the reclining seats as you are whisked to your hidden retreat.

In fact, if you have somehow become partially incapacitated, perhaps the mayhem on the streets has led to your getting shot or knifed, using a self-driving car is perfect since you aren't readily able to drive the car anyway and you've instead got the AI to do the driving for you.

Yay!

Excuse me, I don't mean to pop the balloon on this fanciful hope, but as survivalists are oft to say, you've got to face the reality when reality hits you in the face.

Let's go over the many downsides of trying to use a self-driving car in this particular use case.

First, assuming that driverless cars are owned by large companies and not by individuals (which, I dispute here, but let's go with the assumption for now), you as a survivalist are going to be dependent upon finding a driverless car and getting it to take you to some distant locale.

If the shucks have really hit the fan, does it seem realistic to expect that driverless cars are simply going to be roaming around and letting people take rides wherever they want to go?

Doubtful.

The fleet owner might decide to call their fleet to their home base and maybe allow only their own employees to use them in the emerging emergency situation unraveling (that's a nice perk!).

Or, the company might decide to stop all the driverless cars from taking on any rides at all. The self-driving cars could be summarily stopped at wherever each happens to be, and without the electronic approval from HQ, those driverless cars are multi-ton deadweights.

Even if the fleet owner wants the driverless cars to be giving rides, it could be that electronic networks are messed-up and perhaps the self-driving cars have been programmed that unless they are able to connect with the HQ cloud, they aren't to proceed other than undertaking ride requests within a narrow distance or locale.

For Level 4 self-driving cars, there's another somewhat unpublicized constraint that you need to consider too.

With Level 4, a driverless car has a pre-defined Operational Design Domain (ODD), which means that the self-driving car is only supposed to function within a set of established conditions. For example, a driverless car might only work when the weather is sunny and only drive in a pre-mapped city, otherwise, it isn't capable of driving the car.

Level 4 self-driving cars that are made by different automakers will each have their own idiosyncratic set of ODD's.

Thus, you might get seemingly lucky and manage to flag down an available Level 4 driverless car when you are on the verge of your escape, but upon telling the AI to proceed to your out-of-town retreat, the AI might respond that unfortunately, it is a location beyond it's ODD and cannot drive you there.

Imagine your chagrin that you managed to actually find a roaming driverless car, which might be scarce during the chaos that's ensuing, and then find out that the furthest it will take you is the nearby grocery store (at which people are already in a crazed frenzy and clearing the shelves of all food and provisions).

In short, it would seem like you are going to be out-of-luck because you don't own the driverless car, and you have become entirely dependent upon someone else, a fleet owner, allowing you to use a self-driving car for your escape, yet this presents numerous hurdles and problems when the time comes to make your move.

That's antithetical to being a survivalist.

No weak links in the chain.

Pretend for a moment that you have available a Level 5 self-driving car. Assume further that it is at your disposal all the time and ready for your town-leaving trek (I'm going with this, though it is especially farfetched).

Guess what?

The official definition for Level 5 is that off-road driving is considered out-of-scope.

That's right, there is no requirement that a Level 5 must be able to drive beyond the everyday roads and highways. It might be able to do so, but there's no stated requirement that it must be able to do so.

Therefore, your Level 5 self-driving car that's been sitting in your garage and waiting for the day of action, could refuse to go off-road when you get underway and confront such a need, and end up leaving you stranded or unable to reach your distant and woods hidden or middle-of-the-desert underground bunker.

Darn.

You might be thinking that you could just hack the Level 4 or Level 5 driverless car and get it to do your bidding. Reprogram the darned thing to do what you say, such as go outside the defined ODD of the Level 4 or go off-road as a Level 5.

Presumably, the self-driving car makers have put in place a bunch of impenetrable cyber-security barriers to prevent people from fiddling with the on-board computers (for more about the impending cyber-hacking that will surely aim at self-driving cars, see this piece here).

If you can readily hack the AI for the escape, it would imply that people could be hacking driverless cars all the time. Hopefully, the AI and on-board processors aren't going to be so readily overturned.

As you can plainly see, driverless cars present many qualms as an escape vehicle.

The good thing about conventional cars is that you don't need to argue with a computer processor or an AI system and can pretty much commandeer a car when needed.

A survivalist that has set aside their Bug-Out Vehicle might be prepared to hotwire another car at random, doing so if they aren't able to get access to their BOV (maybe it's parked at home, and they are currently at work). In the chaos of the societal uprising, nobody is likely to notice someone stealing a car.

With self-driving cars, there isn't going to be the equivalent ability to commandeer the vehicle.

Plus, most of the driverless car makers are going to remove the driving controls entirely, such as the steering wheel and the pedals, wanting to make sure that no human can drive the car. The driving controls are hidden underneath the hood and will be controlled exclusively by the AI system.

Conclusion

There's more bad news to bear.

The odds are that the rooftop of the driverless car is going to contain a raft of delicate sensors such as LIDAR and cameras. These are essential for the AI to drive the car.

There might not be any ready means to pile your stuff onto the roof of the vehicle. Trying to do so could likely harm the sensors and it would render the AI unable to drive the car.

Another facet involves fuel.

Self-driving cars are most likely going to be EV's, which makes a lot of sense since the electronic sensors and on-board computers are going to be gobbling up lots of electrical power.

Storing extra gasoline for the day of reckoning for a conventional combustion engine car is somewhat easy to do (though not necessarily safe), while trying to somehow store "extra" electrical power is a lot more challenging.

You might also consider that EV's to-date can't go long distances without running out of fuel. There also aren't a lot of EV charging stations, especially if you are heading to a remote location.

And, the odds are too that any happenstance charging stations might not be working anyway, not once the electrical grid gets cut off during the societal anarchy.

On and on the list goes of reasons why a self-driving car is not going to be your best buddy in a crisis.

Some pundits that favor driverless cars have been clamoring that we ought to ban all conventional cars and have only driverless cars allowed on our roadways.

The logic is somewhat sound in that if you believe that self-driving cars will reduce the number of annual deaths and injuries due to driving cars, you might be able to save lives by getting rid of conventional human-driven cars.

Today's society takes a dim view of such a proposition for a number of reasons (the most obvious being that we don't yet have true self-driving cars that are ready for widespread use and therefore we are still reliant on conventional cars).

Someday, besides everyday self-driving cars being prevalent, we are likely to also have off-roading self-driving cars, which might then be a potential "solution" for those that desire or might need that kind of rough road and back-of-the-woods going capability.

Meanwhile, back to the present and the upcoming future.

There are many people that insist it is their gosh-darned right to drive a car and you are not going to take away that privilege without a fight.

A survivalist might insist that you'll take away their conventional car when you've pried their cold dead hands from their steering wheel.

Now that I've explored the reasons why a driverless car is not an apt Bug-Out Vehicle, I think you can understand why there are survivalists hanging onto their conventional car for dear life.

It could indeed spell the difference between their life or death, once the shenanigans hit the fan.

APPENDIX

APPENDIX A

TEACHING WITH THIS MATERIAL

The material in this book can be readily used either as a supplemental to other content for a class, or it can also be used as a core set of textbook material for a specialized class. Classes where this material is most likely used include any classes at the college or university level that want to augment the class by offering thought provoking and educational essays about AI and self-driving cars.

In particular, here are some aspects for class use:

o   <u>Computer Science</u>. Studying AI, autonomous vehicles, etc.

o   <u>Business</u>. Exploring technology and it adoption for business.

o   <u>Sociology</u>. Sociological views on the adoption and advancement of technology.

Specialized classes at the undergraduate and graduate level can also make use of this material.

For each chapter, consider whether you think the chapter provides material relevant to your course topic. There is plenty of opportunity to get the students thinking about the topic and force them to decide whether they agree or disagree with the points offered and positions taken. I would also encourage you to have the students do additional research beyond the chapter material presented (I provide next some suggested assignments they can do).

RESEARCH ASSIGNMENTS ON THESE TOPICS

Your students can find background material on these topics, doing so in various business and technical publications. I list below the top ranked AI related journals. For business publications, I would suggest the usual culprits such as the Harvard Business Review, Forbes, Fortune, WSJ, and the like.

Here are some suggestions of homework or projects that you could assign to students:

a) Assignment for foundational AI research topic: Research and prepare a paper and a presentation on a specific aspect of Deep AI, Machine Learning, ANN, etc. The paper should cite at least 3 reputable sources. Compare and contrast to what has been stated in this book.

b) Assignment for the Self-Driving Car topic: Research and prepare a paper and Self-Driving Cars. Cite at least 3 reputable sources and analyze the characterizations. Compare and contrast to what has been stated in this book.

c) Assignment for a Business topic: Research and prepare a paper and a presentation on businesses and advanced technology. What is hot, and what is not? Cite at least 3 reputable sources. Compare and contrast to the depictions in this book.

d) Assignment to do a Startup: Have the students prepare a paper about how they might startup a business in this realm. They must submit a sound Business Plan for the startup. They could also be asked to present their Business Plan and so should also have a presentation deck to coincide with it.

You can certainly adjust the aforementioned assignments to fit to your particular needs and the class structure. You'll notice that I ask for 3 reputable cited sources for the paper writing based assignments. I usually steer students toward "reputable" publications, since otherwise they will cite some oddball source that has no credentials other than that they happened to write something and post it onto the Internet. You can define "reputable" in whatever way you prefer, for example some faculty think Wikipedia is not reputable while others believe it is reputable and allow students to cite it.

The reason that I usually ask for at least 3 citations is that if the student only does one or two citations they usually settle on whatever they happened to find the fastest. By requiring three citations, it usually seems to force them to look around, explore, and end-up probably finding five or more, and then whittling it down to 3 that they will actually use.

I have not specified the length of their papers, and leave that to you to tell the students what you prefer. For each of those assignments, you could end-up with a short one to two pager, or you could do a dissertation length paper. Base the length on whatever best fits for your class, and the credit amount of the assignment within the context of the other grading metrics you'll be using for the class.

I mention in the assignments that they are to do a paper and prepare a presentation. I usually try to get students to present their work. This is a good practice for what they will do in the business world. Most of the time, they will be required to prepare an analysis and present it. If you don't have the class time or inclination to have the students present, then you can of course cut out the aspect of them putting together a presentation.

If you want to point students toward highly ranked journals in AI, here's a list of the top journals as reported by *various citation counts sources* (this list changes year to year):

- Communications of the ACM
- Artificial Intelligence
- Cognitive Science
- IEEE Transactions on Pattern Analysis and Machine Intelligence
- Foundations and Trends in Machine Learning
- Journal of Memory and Language
- Cognitive Psychology
- Neural Networks
- IEEE Transactions on Neural Networks and Learning Systems
- IEEE Intelligent Systems
- Knowledge-based Systems

GUIDE TO USING THE CHAPTERS

For each of the chapters, I provide next some various ways to use the chapter material. You can assign the tasks as individual homework assignments, or the tasks can be used with team projects for the class. You can easily layout a series of assignments, such as indicating that the students are to do item "a" below for say Chapter 1, then "b" for the next chapter of the book, and so on.

a) What is the main point of the chapter and describe in your own words the significance of the topic,

b) Identify at least two aspects in the chapter that you agree with, and support your concurrence by providing at least one other outside researched item as support; make sure to explain your basis for disagreeing with the aspects,

c) Identify at least two aspects in the chapter that you disagree with, and support your disagreement by providing at least one other outside researched item as support; make sure to explain your basis for disagreeing with the aspects,

d) Find an aspect that was not covered in the chapter, doing so by conducting outside research, and then explain how that aspect ties into the chapter and what significance it brings to the topic,

e) Interview a specialist in industry about the topic of the chapter, collect from them their thoughts and opinions, and readdress the chapter by citing your source and how they compared and contrasted to the material,

f) Interview a relevant academic professor or researcher in a college or university about the topic of the chapter, collect from them their thoughts and opinions, and readdress the chapter by citing your source and how they compared and contrasted to the material,

g) Try to update a chapter by finding out the latest on the topic, and ascertain whether the issue or topic has now been solved or whether it is still being addressed, explain what you come up with.

The above are all ways in which you can get the students of your class involved in considering the material of a given chapter. You could mix things up by having one of those above assignments per each week, covering the chapters over the course of the semester or quarter.

As a reminder, here are the chapters of the book and you can select whichever chapters you find most valued for your particular class:

Chapter Title

1 Eliot Framework for AI Self-Driving Cars

2 Leaving A Tip and AI Self-Driving Cars

3 Digital Nudging and AI Self-Driving Cars

4 Carpool Lanes and AI Self-Driving Cars

5 Sleep Solving and AI Self-Driving Cars

6 Nostradamus and AI Self-Driving Cars

7 Advanced Driving and AI Self-Driving Cars

8 Cybertruck Windows Shattered Mystery

9 Artificial Stupidity and AI Self-Driving Cars

10 Revenue Estimates Of AI Self-Driving Cars

11 Survivalists and AI Self-Driving Cars

12 Self-Driving Trucks And Self-Driving Cars

Companion Book By This Author

Advances in AI and Autonomous Vehicles: Cybernetic Self-Driving Cars

Practical Advances in Artificial Intelligence (AI) and Machine Learning

by

Dr. Lance B. Eliot, MBA, PhD

This title is available via Amazon and other book sellers

Companion Book By This Author

Self-Driving Cars: "The Mother of All AI Projects"

by Dr. Lance B. Eliot, MBA, PhD

This title is available via Amazon and other book sellers

This title is available via Amazon and other book sellers

Companion Book By This Author

New Advances in AI Autonomous Driverless Cars Self-Driving Cars

by Dr. Lance B. Eliot, MBA, PhD

Chapter Title

This title is available via Amazon and other book sellers

Companion Book By This Author

Introduction to
Driverless Self-Driving Cars

by Dr. Lance B. Eliot, MBA, PhD

This title is available via Amazon and other book sellers

Companion Book By This Author

Autonomous Vehicle Driverless Self-Driving Cars and Artificial Intelligence

by Dr. Lance B. Eliot, MBA, PhD

This title is available via Amazon and other book sellers

Companion Book By This Author

Transformative Artificial Intelligence Driverless Self-Driving Cars

by Dr. Lance B. Eliot, MBA, PhD

This title is available via Amazon and other book sellers

Companion Book By This Author

Disruptive Artificial Intelligence and Driverless Self-Driving Cars

by Dr. Lance B. Eliot, MBA, PhD

Chapter Title

This title is available via Amazon and other book sellers

Companion Book By This Author

State-of-the-Art
AI Driverless Self-Driving Cars

by Dr. Lance B. Eliot, MBA, PhD

Chapter Title

This title is available via Amazon and other book sellers

Companion Book By This Author

Top Trends in
AI Self-Driving Cars

by Dr. Lance B. Eliot, MBA, PhD

This title is available via Amazon and other book sellers

Companion Book By This Author

***AI Innovations
and Self-Driving Cars***

by Dr. Lance B. Eliot, MBA, PhD

<u>Chapter Title</u>

This title is available via Amazon and other book sellers

Crucial Advances for
AI Self-Driving Cars

by Dr. Lance B. Eliot, MBA, PhD

<u>Chapter Title</u>

This title is available via Amazon and other book sellers

Companion Book By This Author

Sociotechnical Insights and AI Driverless Cars

by Dr. Lance B. Eliot, MBA, PhD

This title is available via Amazon and other book sellers

Companion Book By This Author

Pioneering Advances for AI Driverless Cars

by Dr. Lance B. Eliot, MBA, PhD

This title is available via Amazon and other book sellers

Companion Book By This Author

Leading Edge Trends for AI Driverless Cars

by Dr. Lance B. Eliot, MBA, PhD

This title is available via Amazon and other book sellers

Companion Book By This Author

The Cutting Edge of AI Autonomous Cars

by Dr. Lance B. Eliot, MBA, PhD

Chapter Title

This title is available via Amazon and other book sellers

This title is available via Amazon and other book sellers

Revolutionary Innovations of AI Self-Driving Cars

by Dr. Lance B. Eliot, MBA, PhD

Chapter Title

<u>Companion Book By This Author</u>

AI Self-Driving Cars
Breakthroughs

by Dr. Lance B. Eliot, MBA, PhD

<u>Chapter Title</u>

This title is available via Amazon and other book sellers

Companion Book By This Author

Trailblazing Trends for
AI Self-Driving Cars

by Dr. Lance B. Eliot, MBA, PhD

This title is available via Amazon and other book sellers

Companion Book By This Author

Ingenious Strides for
AI Driverless Cars

by Dr. Lance B. Eliot, MBA, PhD

This title is available via Amazon and other book sellers

Companion Book By This Author

AI Self-Driving Cars
Inventiveness

by Dr. Lance B. Eliot, MBA, PhD

This title is available via Amazon and other book sellers

Visionary Secrets of AI Driverless Cars

by Dr. Lance B. Eliot, MBA, PhD

Chapter Title

This title is available via Amazon and other book sellers

Companion Book By This Author

Spearheading
AI Self-Driving Cars

by Dr. Lance B. Eliot, MBA, PhD

This title is available via Amazon and other book sellers

Companion Book By This Author

Spurring
AI Self-Driving Cars

by Dr. Lance B. Eliot, MBA, PhD

This title is available via Amazon and other book sellers

Lance B. Eliot

Companion Book By This Author

Avant-Garde
AI Driverless Cars

by Dr. Lance B. Eliot, MBA, PhD

Chapter Title

This title is available via Amazon and other book sellers

<u>Companion Book By This Author</u>

AI Self-Driving Cars
Evolvement

by Dr. Lance B. Eliot, MBA, PhD

<u>Chapter Title</u>

This title is available via Amazon and other book sellers

<u>Companion Book By This Author</u>

AI Driverless Cars
Chrysalis

by Dr. Lance B. Eliot, MBA, PhD

This title is available via Amazon and other book sellers

Companion Book By This Author

Boosting
AI Autonomous Cars
by Dr. Lance B. Eliot, MBA, PhD

This title is available via Amazon and other book sellers

Companion Book By This Author

AI Self-Driving Cars Trendsetting

by Dr. Lance B. Eliot, MBA, PhD

This title is available via Amazon and other book sellers

<u>Companion Book By This Author</u>

AI Autonomous Cars
Forefront

by Dr. Lance B. Eliot, MBA, PhD

This title is available via Amazon and other book sellers

Companion Book By This Author

AI Autonomous Cars Emergence

by Dr. Lance B. Eliot, MBA, PhD

Chapter Title

1 Eliot Framework for AI Self-Driving Cars

2 Dropping Off Riders and AI Self-Driving Cars

3 Add-On Kits Drive.AI and AI Self-Driving Cars

4 Boeing 737 Emergency Flaw and AI Self-Driving Cars

5 Spinout Tesla Autopilot and AI Self-Driving Cars

6 Earthquakes and AI Self-Driving Cars

7 Ford Mobility Lab and AI Self-Driving Cars

8 Apollo 11 Error Code and AI Self-Driving Cars

9 Nuro Self-Driving Vehicle and AI Self-Driving Cars

10 Safety First (SaFAD) Aptiv and AI Self-Driving Cars

11 Brainjacking Neuralink and AI Self-Driving Cars

12 Storming Area 51 and AI Self-Driving Cars

13 Riding Inside An AI Self-Driving Car

14 ACES Acronym and AI Self-Driving Cars

15 Kids Bike Riding and AI Self-Driving Cars

16 LIDAR Not Doomed and AI Self-Driving Cars

This title is available via Amazon and other book sellers

Companion Book By This Author

AI Autonomous Cars Progress

by Dr. Lance B. Eliot, MBA, PhD

This title is available via Amazon and other book sellers

<u>Companion Book By This Author</u>

AI Self-Driving Cars
Prognosis
by Dr. Lance B. Eliot, MBA, PhD

This title is available via Amazon and other book sellers

Companion Book By This Author

AI Self-Driving Cars
Momentum

by Dr. Lance B. Eliot, MBA, PhD

This title is available via Amazon and other book sellers

<u>Companion Book By This Author</u>

AI Self-Driving Cars
Headway

by Dr. Lance B. Eliot, MBA, PhD

<u>Chapter Title</u>

This title is available via Amazon and other book sellers

Companion Book By This Author

AI Self-Driving Cars Vicissitude

by Dr. Lance B. Eliot, MBA, PhD

Chapter Title

This title is available via Amazon and other book sellers

ABOUT THE AUTHOR

Dr. Lance B. Eliot, MBA, PhD is the CEO of Techbruim, Inc. and Executive Director of the Cybernetic AI Self-Driving Car Institute and has over twenty years of industry experience including serving as a corporate officer in a billion dollar firm and was a partner in a major executive services firm. He is also a serial entrepreneur having founded, ran, and sold several high-tech related businesses. He previously hosted the popular radio show *Technotrends* that was also available on American Airlines flights via their in-flight audio program. Author or co-author of a dozen books and over 400 articles, he has made appearances on CNN, and has been a frequent speaker at industry conferences.

A former professor at the University of Southern California (USC), he founded and led an innovative research lab on Artificial Intelligence in Business. Known as the "AI Insider" his writings on AI advances and trends has been widely read and cited. He also previously served on the faculty of the University of California Los Angeles (UCLA), and was a visiting professor at other major universities. He was elected to the International Board of the Society for Information Management (SIM), a prestigious association of over 3,000 high-tech executives worldwide.

He has performed extensive community service, including serving as Senior Science Adviser to the Vice Chair of the Congressional Committee on Science & Technology. He has served on the Board of the OC Science & Engineering Fair (OCSEF), where he is also has been a Grand Sweepstakes judge, and likewise served as a judge for the Intel International SEF (ISEF). He served as the Vice Chair of the Association for Computing Machinery (ACM) Chapter, a prestigious association of computer scientists. Dr. Eliot has been a shark tank judge for the USC Mark Stevens Center for Innovation on start-up pitch competitions, and served as a mentor for several incubators and accelerators in Silicon Valley and Silicon Beach. He served on several Boards and Committees at USC, including having served on the Marshall Alumni Association (MAA) Board in Southern California.

Dr. Eliot holds a PhD from USC, MBA, and Bachelor's in Computer Science, and earned the CDP, CCP, CSP, CDE, and CISA certifications. Born and raised in Southern California, and having traveled and lived internationally, he enjoys scuba diving, surfing, and sailing.

ADDENDUM

AI Self-Driving Cars Vicissitude

Practical Advances in Artificial Intelligence (AI) and Machine Learning

By
Dr. Lance B. Eliot, MBA, PhD

———

For supplemental materials of this book, visit:
www.ai-selfdriving-cars.guru

For special orders of this book, contact:
LBE Press Publishing
Email: LBE.Press.Publishing@gmail.com

www.ingramcontent.com/pod-product-compliance
Lightning Source LLC
Chambersburg PA
CBHW051047050326
40690CB00006B/630